My Year with God

Sydney / Mom,

Thank you so much for having me this weekend.

So excited to spend time with you and the family.

I thought this book was really good and wanted to share!

Love you,
Julia

My Year with God
Faith for Doubters

Svend Brinkmann

Translated by Tam McTurk

polity

First published in Danish as *Mit år med Gud*, © Svend Brinkmann and
Gyldendal, Copenhagen, 2021. Published by agreement with Gyldendal Group
Agency
This English edition © Polity Press, 2022

Translated by Tam McTurk

Polity Press
65 Bridge Street
Cambridge CB2 1UR, UK

Polity Press
111 River Street
Hoboken, NJ 07030, USA

ISBN-13: 978-1-5095-5271-9
ISBN-13: 978-1-5095-5272-6 (pb)

A catalogue record for this book is available from the British Library.

Library of Congress Control Number: 2022934660

Typeset in 11 on 14 pt Fournier by
Cheshire Typesetting Ltd, Cuddington, Cheshire
Printed and bound in Great Britain by TJ Books Ltd, Padstow, Cornwall

The publisher has used its best endeavours to ensure that the URLs for external
websites referred to in this book are correct and active at the time of going to
press. However, the publisher has no responsibility for the websites and can make
no guarantee that a site will remain live or that the content is or will remain
appropriate.

Every effort has been made to trace all copyright holders, but if any have been
overlooked the publisher will be pleased to include any necessary credits in any
subsequent reprint or edition.

For further information on Polity, visit our website:
politybooks.com

Contents

Preface

I have been interested in religion and faith ever since I was a small child. 'Does God exist? If there's a god, it would change everything!' was the way my mind worked back then. 'So why are we not all thrashing it out passionately until we settle the matter once and for all?', I mused. It was baffling. Surely this was one of life's biggest questions?

Despite harbouring thoughts like these for so long, I have never reached a definitive conclusion. At times, I have really wanted to believe, but not found it in me. At others, I have looked askance at the faithful: what is it that makes them capable of believing such incredible things? Is it faith or delusion? Or perhaps there is something wrong with me? I do not believe in spirits, gods, miracles, resurrection or eternal life. I am deeply sceptical about all things spiritual, alternative or with the merest hint of the New Age. And yet, I am deeply fascinated by religion. There is just no getting away from it.

With all these questions ringing in my ears, I chose to spend a year of my life looking at what faith and religion are – and can be – in the modern world. The idea was to find out whether the religious dimension to life might have relevance to someone like me, a scientist from a secular background. What can religion be for those of us who do not believe that there is more between heaven and earth than we might imagine?

Each month, I looked at a different question to do with faith and religion. I addressed each one with every ounce of curiosity and openness I could muster, seeking to cast off personal prejudices and give God a chance – at least for a year. I hoped that my diary would forge a path somewhere between fundamentalism and outright rejection of religion, that I would be open-minded and not become bogged down in either of the two all-too-familiar trenches from which people often fight it out over these questions.

No matter which way you look at it, the fact remains that the vast majority of people have always professed some kind of religious faith or another. Indeed, studies suggest that is still the case for more than 80 per cent of humanity,[1] so it is highly probable that you, the reader, are either religious or at least open to the concept. Contrary to a great deal of twentieth-century thinking, the world does not seem to be evolving away from religion and towards atheism. Not believing in a god of some kind remains a minority position. For better or worse, faith seems to be here to stay, and although the questions raised in this book are ones that aroused my personal curiosity, I hope they will help believers and non-believers alike to come to a better understanding of each other. Perhaps they are not as far apart as they often think.

The book can be read from start to finish. It was written chronologically, in diary form, and, to some extent, the chapters build on each other. Having said that, it should also be possible to jump around and read about questions and themes of particular interest. Where appropriate, I have drawn on previous works that sprang to mind when contemplating the issue at hand.

I would like to thank the patient readers who provided helpful feedback as I was writing the book: Kåre Egholm Pedersen, Christian Hjortkjær, Lene Tanggaard and Thomas Aastrup Rømer – two theologians, a psychologist and an associate professor of pedagogical philosophy. You made important and challenging points and I have tried my best to follow up on them. Thanks are also due to my ever-helpful editor, Anne Weinkouff, for being open to my ideas and providing invaluable support all the way from the idea stage to publication. It is great to have an editor who is on the same wavelength as the author's thinking and language. For the English edition of the book, I would like to thank everyone at Polity, especially Inès Boxman and Louise Knight, and Tam McTurk who provided a wonderful translation. Thanks also to my family – Ellen, Karl, Jens and Signe – for listening and discussing each of the monthly questions with me. Conversation is perhaps the best medium for debates about faith and philosophy, so I am grateful to all of those with whom I have discussed existential matters over the years. Finally, I would like to dedicate the book to my mother, who always listened to all my questions – including the ones to which there are no answers.

January

Why a book about God?

2 January

My childhood musings about whether there is a god weren't just for fun. After all, the existence of a deity would imply some kind of order in the universe that we – humankind – didn't create. It would mean a supreme being who might have a plan for our lives, whether we like it or not. It would provide some kind of meaning and purpose to life. It might even mean there's an afterlife – at least if God is indeed omnipotent, omnibenevolent and wants the best for us. But, purely logically, the existence of a god also throws up the less appealing possibility that we risk eternal damnation for the sins we commit in this life – an idea guaranteed to give any child sleepless nights.

Maybe it's all the other way around if there's no God? Maybe we have to define the meaning of life ourselves and endow it with a significance that stretches beyond mere physical existence. But what might that be in a universe in which physics, chemistry and biology explain everything, and nothing lasts forever? Ultimately, is meaning even possible without a God?

According to the statistics, I have now lived over half of my life without answering the question I first asked myself as a child. And I'm pretty sure I'm not alone. Many people are religious, of course – even in a relatively secular country such as Denmark, where I was born and still live. Many also call themselves atheists and absolutely reject any belief in a supreme power. But then many of us find ourselves somewhere in between these two poles. Do we have to choose a side? And if so, how?

Like the vast majority of Danes, I was baptised and confirmed in the established Lutheran Church and would probably be described by some as 'culturally Christian' – but I can't purport to believe in God. He didn't really play a role in my childhood home. We didn't say grace before meals or pray before bed, and only went to church for baptisms, confirmations, weddings and funerals. If we did talk about religion, it was implicit that faith was irrational and that, ultimately, the world could be explained scientifically.

The funny thing is that I can't say with certainty that I *don't* believe in God either. Atheism has always seemed to me to be a bit too definitive a position in a world so mysterious that some astronomers are religious, and famous physicists like Stephen Hawking and Holger Bech Nielsen discuss the possibility of a God without scoffing at the concept – even though the former did dismiss God as an unnecessary hypothesis, and the latter operates with a concept of 'God' in quotation marks. Years ago, when I signed up for Facebook and was asked my religious views, I wrote 'agnostic' – the slightly dull, fence-sitting position of not really having faith but leaving the door slightly ajar just in case. Agnosticism implies that mere mortals are not in a position to judge whether there is a higher being. Much like the ant has no way of knowing that humans exist due to the limited intellectual capacity of the species, according to agnosticism, human ants are in much the same position when it comes to positing the existence or non-existence of a deity.

I have a deep-rooted fear of religious fundamentalism, in the sense of justifying attitudes to politics, ethics or life by calling it God's will. But dogmatic atheism seems almost as bad to me – not because atheism is a religion, as some of its opponents like to claim (no, lack of religion really *is* the opposite of having religion), but because I find it fairly unimaginative. It suggests that the materialistic interpretation of the world of the last few centuries, which leaves no room for the divine, is the ultimate truth. How do we know for sure? 'We' don't. At least not if 'we' means humanity as a whole, because the vast majority of us have always professed some form of faith – and still do.

This year, I am going to give God a chance. My uneasy relationship with religion has gone on for long enough. What does it mean to believe? How do you start? What is the relationship between personal faith and organized religion? Does finding religion change your life? Does a secular outlook on life leave any room for religion? What use is faith? Does it make you more moral? These are some of the questions I want to explore. I have no way of knowing what the outcome will be. I can't promise to come out as a believer and change my Facebook profile. Right now, in fact, I'd say that's pretty unlikely, but I do promise to commit myself wholeheartedly and openly to the religious dimension. I will look at faith in a sincere and inquisitive manner without jumping to conclusions, and readers will be able to follow the process as I, hopefully, become wiser.

While it was my choice to explore religion and write a book about it, I don't think people choose to be religious any more than we choose to fall in love. But perhaps an open and enquiring mind makes us more receptive to the impulse – just like falling in love. This is one of the things I hope to find out this year. I readily concede that the whole venture has a somewhat artificial air. I expect most people become religious when they find themselves in an existentially borderline situation or face a major crisis, such as losing a loved one or being diagnosed with a terminal illness. 'There are no atheists in foxholes', as the saying goes. Take, for example, the Danish author Puk Qvortrup's moving book *Into a Star*, about how, as the pregnant mother of a young toddler, she suddenly lost her husband and the father of her children. She had never believed in God, but

when her husband was on life support in hospital, Puk
found herself praying:

> I was surprised to see my hands clutched to my chest and
> hear myself whisper: Dear God, please, please listen to
> me. We haven't spoken before because I don't believe in
> you. But this isn't about me; it's about Lasse. Now's the
> time to show me you exist. Lasse is about to be a father
> again; he has so much to live for. We need him. Show
> mercy.[1]

But no mercy was shown. Lasse didn't come back round.
And therein lies one of the classic religious conundrums:
why would God allow innocent people to die far too young
and cause grief to so many others?

I have never suffered a devastating loss like Puk Qvortrup.
I'm also well aware that I live a privileged and secure life
with a loving family in a reasonably well-run country. I have
no obvious reason for giving God a chance. Maybe I should
wait until a crisis hits – because sooner or later, they always
do. I could also approach the question from the opposite
perspective: I may not currently be facing any of life's great
dramas, but they come to all mere mortals at some point, so
perhaps it would be good to think about faith before they
strike.

That is one reason to make a start – so that I'm not totally
lacking in religious resources when the day comes that I
need to deploy them. (I am already having doubts about
my approach: *deploy* sounds too instrumental, although it
is one of my considerations.) The second reason is so that
nobody can say I have turned to the religious dimension
out of sheer desperation. Quite the contrary, in fact. I do
so out of sincere interest. One oft-cited objection to faith is
that it acts as some kind of comfort blanket for people who
need solace and hope – one implication of which is that
religion is, in fact, just an illusion, something for the weak.

Given how many people are believers – and the historical
influence of religion on virtually every aspect of all human
cultures – I find the comfort-blanket critique lacking in
credibility. Maybe faith fulfils that function for some, but
it has many other functions as well. Besides, what's wrong
with comfort blankets? Surely no one would dismiss somebody like Puk Qvortrup, who turns to God – in whom she
doesn't even really believe – out of pure despair? Not me,
at any rate.

I'm writing this on an intercity train speeding from one
end of the country to the other. It's a brand new year, and
no one yet knows what it will bring. My journey with God
begins now, on the second day of the year, and will continue
until the end of December. Family, friends and colleagues
may rest assured that I'm unlikely to cast off my worldview
based on physics, cosmology, evolutionary theory, psychology and whatever else we think we know about the universe,
the planet, life and humankind. It would take something
completely unexpected for that to happen. It would be a bit
like being a different person – so closely are my views on life
linked to a scientific understanding of the world.

Nor do I have the remotest intention of turning into a
hermit in a forest or desert, or retreating to an ashram in
India in search of mysticism. I can also guarantee readers
that I won't become a creationist and believe that God, as
an intelligent designer, created the world once and for all,
mere millennia ago. I have always thought such a literal
interpretation of the Bible, which fabricates some kind of
competition between religion and science, is totally wrong.
Partly because, if that were the case, science would always
prevail over religion due to its empirical methodology and
ability to predict outcomes, but also because it turns religion into something that it is not. Religion and science are
not parallel paths to enlightenment, competing to see which
has the deepest understanding of the same issues. They
deal with different kinds of issues. They are about different

things. And that is the basis for my approach to this book and the year ahead.

But why a book? Why reach out to other people? Why not just search my soul for traces of faith and not bother other people? The answer is that I think many others feel the same. A lot of us are secularized, culturally Christian agnostics, and it would be good for us to have a collective discussion about the nature of faith and religion and the impact they can and should have on modern human life in a secular society. Judging by the sheer number of interviews, radio broadcasts and TV documentaries on these topics at the moment, there really does seem to be a widespread and genuine interest in such a discussion, and I want to play my part in it.

I have done a lot of work on the legacy from antiquity and the enduring significance to this day of Greek thinking. I have drawn on what might be called the legacy of Athens – the thread in the history of ideas that began with the ancient Greek philosophers and continued up to the Renaissance and into the Enlightenment, which we might also call humanism. In this tradition, humans are rational, ethical and possess an innate dignity that makes us deserving of respect. However, there is also what might be called the legacy of Jerusalem. The Christian heritage has been equally essential to human self-understanding and to society in our part of the world. As the historian Tom Holland recently concluded, Christianity even 'created the Western consciousness'.[2]

With these thoughts in mind, one of my goals with this book will be to supplement 'Athens' with 'Jerusalem' – the intensely rational Greek with the humbler, more devout Christian. Religion has been a bit of a blind spot in my work – not because I didn't want to accord it significance, but because my focus was elsewhere. Although my books have not directly addressed God, they have nevertheless addressed many of the same ethical and existential questions around which Christianity and other world religions revolve, and to which they offer answers. So, the time has come to look God in the eye. For a year anyway.

5 January

Home again after a few days in Copenhagen. Unfortunately, work won out on the long train ride and marking exam papers took precedence over reflections on faith and religion. It wasn't exactly a religious experience. But I have managed to spend some time on the question of why I think it's important that I write this book. Am I actually religious without knowing it? Finding the answer to that is one of my first priorities. After all, if I'm already a believer, what's the point in making a fuss about becoming one?

When discussing religion with colleagues, I have occasionally cited a remark by Ludwig Wittgenstein, perhaps the greatest philosopher of the twentieth century. It was he who laid the foundations for the discussion about the philosophy of language that took centre stage in the latter half of the century and showed that language isn't a single thing but consists of myriad language games used for different purposes. One consequence of this line of thought is that religious language is not the same as scientific language. Wittgenstein once said that he was not a religious man but couldn't help looking at every problem from a religious point of view. This is largely how I think of myself. As mentioned previously, when asked whether I believe in God, I don't really know how to respond – what does it even mean to 'believe in God'? Nevertheless, I think there are many insights about life to be gained from theology and religious philosophy. I also really like visiting churches and graveyards – partly for aesthetic reasons, but also because they strike a chord somewhere on my emotional scale that few other places reach. I know many other non-believers feel the same way. Does this indicate that I have some kind of impulse to believe?

An example of my ambivalent attitude to religion: in 2018, the Danish Humanist Society named me its 'Humanist of the Year'. The organization is founded on atheist principles and promotes a society in which all views on life are equal, which would, in effect, water down the role Christianity plays in society. They gave me a nice prize – a beautiful paper collage – and I was grateful for the recognition. Nevertheless, I have to admit to a nagging feeling that the accolade went to the wrong person. I've nothing against being known as a self-avowed humanist in the tradition of Greek philosophy, Renaissance humanism and the Enlightenment ('Athens', as it were), but these days the concept of humanism is often seen as synonymous with atheism, as is the case with the Danish Humanist Society. In his great work on secularization, the philosopher Charles Taylor uses the term 'exclusive humanism', by which he means a humanism that deliberately distances itself from all aims and values beyond human happiness and wellbeing.[3] This atheist form of humanism *excludes* all non-human values, because it doesn't think there is anything else of value other than that which emanates from human happiness. I have my doubts about this philosophy. I sense that there are legitimate discussions to be had about our relationship to life, nature and each other that cannot be accommodated purely within a human horizon. Does this mean that we need faith or religion – perhaps a concept of God? I'm not sure, but it is one of the questions I want to pursue.

8 January

As a research psychologist interested in philosophy, I am used to thinking about a range of different intellectual propositions. What is the relationship between the brain and the psyche? The individual and society? Actions and behaviour? I use scientific tools to tackle these issues. The question is whether the same approach can be used for faith.

Is faith something intellectual, something cognitive? Apart from monks, nuns and others who dedicate their lives to their faith, is it possible to become religious just by thinking about it? By entering into more or less constant meditation on religion? I don't know, but it's something else I hope to find out.

I must admit that one of the consequences of a busy, modern life like mine – one that doesn't revolve around church on Sunday, regular prayer (before meals, at bedtime, etc.) and rules based on religious commandments – is that carving out time and space for religious contemplation requires a conscious decision. As that's the whole point of this project, it's quite ironic that I've not had time to do so yet. Perhaps religion has been marginalized from modern life precisely because so many of us are too busy. No matter your attitude to religion, I think it would be a shame if the reason that people don't believe or don't have the opportunity to engage with these existential questions is simply that they don't have the time.

One thing I have managed to do is start reading Rebecca Newberger Goldstein's *36 Arguments for the Existence of God*, a humorous novel about an atheist lecturer in the psychology of religion who writes a surprise bestseller called *The Varieties of Religious Illusion*.[4] The main character becomes famous as 'the atheist with a soul' because, unlike more dogmatic atheists, he takes religion seriously. I'm only halfway through the book, which I'm actually reading because I am interviewing Goldstein at a festival this summer, but I already see clear echoes of my own project. Goldstein herself is an atheist – with a soul, I think – and her novel contains a copious appendix of works of non-fiction in which she examines 36 pieces of 'proof' of the existence of God and rejects them all. In the Middle Ages, producing such proof and debating it was all the rage, and such theological pondering gave rise to a great deal of deeply fascinating philosophy. The title of the fictional bestseller in Goldstein's book is an allusion to the psychologist William James' major work on comparative religion, *The Varieties of Religious Experience*. James is one of my favourite psychologists and a 'founding father' of American psychology. He lived from 1842 to 1910, a period during which it was quite natural for scientists to study religious experience as a significant dimension of life. Only later, once psychology established itself as a science rooted in the same principles as the natural sciences, which left no room for faith, were such endeavours considered reprehensible.

However, if religion is something we can *think* our way to, and the modern world – from my perspective, at least – doesn't offer rituals that encourage religious openness, then where should we look for God? I've been mulling over whether I've actually ever had an experience that might be characterized as religious. And I think perhaps I have. Not at births, christenings, weddings or funerals. Nor during sex or when drunk. All of these can be intense and moving experiences, but for me they don't trigger anything I would associate with religion.

What I do recall, however, is an experience I had during a family holiday on Sardinia, the Italian island in the Mediterranean where Berlusconi has his holiday home. I went on a boat trip to some caves only accessible from the sea, along with my two sons, who were relatively young at the time. We were in a small boat with other tourists, out on the dark-blue sea, the glorious Mediterranean sun high above us. For some reason or other, I distinctly remember looking at the cliff face ahead and suddenly feeling that everything was OK. Not just with my family, work, health, etc. *Everything* was OK. With the whole world, the universe, the cosmos. The rugged, ancient cliffs, which had been there for millions of years, filled me with a feeling of profound calm and deep meaning. I have had occasional glimpses of something similar before and since, but nothing quite like this. I felt it in my body and mind at the same time – a heavy, insisting and reassuring tranquillity. Everything clicked into place: the sea, the cliffs, the sun, my kids. I don't think I've ever spoken about it before. I find it difficult to put into words what it actually meant. Was it not just a sudden surge of wellbeing that neuroscience or other modern disciplines can explain? Well, I'm pretty sure that all such feelings are based in the brain and central nervous system, but that doesn't mean they can be reduced solely to what happens in the brain (my experience of other people, for example, is similarly based in my brain, but these people also exist outside my consciousness, as separate beings). I can't even say this experience changed me. I didn't become religious or a better person (at some point, I must address whether those two things are actually linked). Nor have I sought to conjure up the sensation again. But I know this type of experience exists, and that, in itself, is gratifying, even if I can't quite explain why. Wittgenstein – who, incidentally, had a notoriously troubled mind – reported similar episodes, which he categorized as a feeling of 'absolute safety':

> I believe the best way of describing it is to say that when I have it *I wonder at the existence of the world.* And I am then inclined to use such phrases as 'how extraordinary that anything should exist' or 'how extraordinary that the world should exist'. I will mention another experience straightaway which I also know and which others of you might be acquainted with: it is, what one might call, the experience of feeling *absolutely* safe. I mean the state of mind in which one is inclined to say, 'I am safe, nothing can injure me whatever happens.'[5]

9 January

I gave a lecture yesterday, after which I had a quick chat with some of the audience. One friendly but insistent woman – in her thirties, I think – wanted to ask me a question.

My talk was about the process of personal formation or edification (which is sometimes described with the German word *Bildung*) and stressed the importance of learning about both the natural sciences and philosophy. The woman asked whether, given all the time I spend thinking about human existence, I felt I was missing out by not believing in God. Did I not regret the absence of something on which I could lean or to which I could 'attach my thoughts'? I think those were the words she used. She explained that she was a believer and that her faith had helped her in life.

I was just about to fire off my standard response to this kind of question: that the existential and ethical questions that interest me can provide meaningful answers without the need to believe in God. For example, ethics don't become meaningless if there is no God behind them; mathematics is no less meaningful in a universe without God. Perhaps God created ethics and maths – perhaps He didn't – but the validity of ethical or mathematical rules is still open to question, entirely independently of the question of whether God exists. My worldview does not, therefore, have to rely on God. That would be my usual answer – and it's still what I think. But I heard myself saying, 'Of course I miss out on something by not believing in God, but you can't force people to believe!'

The woman looked at me with something resembling a mixture of interest and compassion. Luckily, she didn't indulge in the usual response to such situations and start preaching at me. I'm allergic to that. Even if I do envy people who have found meaning in religious faith, I don't welcome their attempts to convince me to believe the same as them. When that happens, I have a childish urge to adopt the opposite view and go full Nietzsche on them! I suspect the only form of evangelizing that might convince me would be to see for myself that the believer's faith had made their life whole, meaningful and worthy of emulation. In other words, their approach ought to be by example rather than seeking to instruct or persuade. Ironically, it is usually those most at peace with themselves who feel the least need to convince others to believe the same as them, while, conversely, the most aggressive evangelists seem to be the ones with the most troubled souls. The urge to spread the truth appears to stem from personal insecurity. But that may, of course, just be my prejudice talking.

Nevertheless, on the way home from the lecture, I kept mulling over the woman's question and my – for me – slightly surprising reply. I was essentially saying that, if faith was something that you can freely choose, then yes, perhaps I would choose to believe! But it is not really a choice. It requires more than a strong will. I can't just choose to believe that my local football team will win the Champions League, or that there's an almighty God who wants the best for me. I just don't *believe* that! How can you *choose* to believe something you don't believe? Believing the unbelievable is a logical impossibility.

As things stand, my sense is that faith could emerge from some form of praxis. Maybe we have to act first and believe afterwards? Or perhaps we can *only* believe in the unbelievable – because if it's something we know, and therefore it's easy to believe, then there's no *need* to have faith in it.

28 January

I'm in Norway giving a series of lectures. Today, it's Trondheim in the beautiful winter sun. As the plane passed over snow-capped mountains on the way here, I tried in vain to conjure up the feeling I remembered from that boat just off Sardinia. The mountains and forests looked so beautiful from above, but ultimately they felt no more magical than a human-made spectacle, like a magnificent fireworks display.

During the flight, I pondered whether this whole 'year with God' project isn't, in fact, just a bit silly. What's wrong with the outlook on life I already have? I've just binge-watched the comedian Ricky Gervais' TV series *After Life*, which was the second most-viewed show on Netflix UK last year. (Well, binge-watched is perhaps a bit of an exaggeration since there were only six episodes.) It's about Tony, a widower, played with great subtlety by Gervais. He is, I suppose, in his late forties – a bit older than me – and has lost his wife to cancer. She was his everything. Life has become meaningless for Tony, and his biggest wish is to end it all as soon as possible. The only thing holding him back is his sense of responsibility for his dog. He also has an ageing father with dementia in a nursing home, whom he visits – albeit reluctantly. He has no children, few friends and colleagues, and we are privy to the almost desperate grief that drives him to cynicism. Why bother doing anything when life is meaningless? Tony decides to do exactly what he wants because he has nothing left to lose. If the consequences become too much, there's always the suicide option, which he considers to be his superpower. He loses it with the postman. He retaliates when two muggers pick on him. He makes unlikely new acquaintances: a junkie and a prostitute. He starts to live more intensely and honestly but is still deeply unhappy.

The series is sad, of course, but it is also highly edifying. Watching it, I thought that it quite accurately encapsulates my existential standpoint. At one point, a colleague confronts Tony, saying that we need to believe in God because, without faith, people will just do whatever they want – perhaps even commit murder and rape. Tony responds that he *is* doing what he wants. He just doesn't want to rape and murder. So he doesn't. It would be really weird to want to do that. And if the only thing stopping people from committing heinous acts was fear of God's punishment, then they wouldn't be particularly moral individuals anyway. Good points and well made, in my opinion.

In one of the most beautiful scenes, Tony visits his wife's grave. He has a new friend – an older widow who regularly visits her husband's grave. She senses Tony's pain and despair. He tells her about his project, about using his superpower to not care about anything and do whatever he wants. The wise widow tells him he's a good man, life is short and that the only thing that ultimately means anything is to be good to others. She points out that life can come to an end at any moment. And there is no afterlife, no prize for good behaviour. Being good to others is the only thing that has any meaning. Her straightforward, beautiful philosophy gave me goosebumps. It sums up secular humanism perfectly. The words have a healing effect on Gervais' tortured character Tony. He is transformed, bit by bit, from a tragic and bitter 'superhero' into a more thoughtful person. He makes amends with the other people in his life – his boss, the irritating colleague and his dad. Towards the end, there's even a hint that he is starting to be receptive to the idea of love again. In some ways, this is all deeply banal, but it is also enormously moving. And the fact that the character is played by Ricky Gervais, who is otherwise known for uncompromising – even offensive – humour means it has even more impact. At the end of the series, it struck me that this is actually how things are. Other people *are* our salvation and give our lives meaning. We don't need God, so why waste time on religion?

But afterwards, I had another thought. What if part of what religion is trying to tell us is precisely that – that there is something almost miraculous about the fact that we exist and are generally able to live together (without raping and murdering each other) in a world that is otherwise dangerous and gruesome, and in which all that lives must die. I realize that this sounds sentimental, but could religion be an attempt to describe the basic conditions for existence in a way that is laden with symbols and metaphors that make those conditions vital and tolerable? That foster solidarity and community (even if that's not always the way religion has worked out in practice)? Perhaps Tony's path back to some semblance of life stems from a form of faith, albeit one that doesn't involve metaphysics or the supernatural? To answer these questions, I will need to look more closely at what religion and faith actually are. That will be the big question next month.

February

What is religion?

3 February

This month, I am going to look at what religion is and at the nature of the relationship between religion and faith. Now, I am no theologian. Nor do I conduct research into religion, so the aim isn't to present a new theory or anything like that. For a layperson like me to attempt that would be nothing short of delusions of grandeur. No, what I want to do is look at whether any of the existing understandings of religion make sense in *my* secular life.

Religion is complex, and the concepts are sometimes confusing. Take the last sentence in the previous paragraph. It would be legitimate to ask whether my life is, in fact, secular. It all comes down to definitions. Nevertheless, for these purposes, *A Secular Age*, the major work by the philosopher Charles Taylor, has provided me with a solid understanding of what is meant by the word 'secular'. Taylor is one of the modern thinkers from whom I have learnt the most. His book covers five centuries of religion. In the Middle Ages, in almost all cultures around the world, not believing in God (or gods in the plural) was virtually impossible. The divine was present and manifest in all things observable in nature and society. This has changed. In the post-Enlightenment age, it seems to be difficult to have faith. Plenty still do, but they are now expected to justify it – their faith is no longer taken for granted. In the past, faith was the basic assumption, and non-believers had to argue their case (often at risk of life and limb). Nowadays, lack of faith is the starting point (at least in my corner of the world) and expressing yourself in religious terms requires justification – and, perhaps, courage.

Viewed in this light, secularization is not about a gradual disappearance of religion as modernization takes hold. At one time, many scientists thought that religion would fade away, but there is little evidence of that happening. In fact, faith and religion are far more resilient in the face of scientific and technological progress than previously envisaged. For Taylor, secularization doesn't mean that faith withers away; rather, it becomes one option among many. In other words, it is possible either to believe or not to believe. It is up to the individual to choose. This is the foundation from which modern humans start posing all of our instrumental questions. Why should I believe? What's in it for me? Will it make my life better? The point is to understand that secularization doesn't mean that faith goes away. Conditions have just changed, making it one of multiple options.

Many of the key problems now facing religion stem from this choice. If faith has become a matter of choice for the secular individual, and yet it is not something we can *choose* (because it's something that comes to us), then we find ourselves facing a paradox. The only way to resolve this is probably through the type of openness that I am trying to practise in this book. We can't just *want* faith. But we can perhaps *want to want* it – that is, be open to the impulse.

4 February

The most apposite word for this openness is, in my view, resonance. I am reading a major work on the subject by the German sociologist Hartmut Rosa. *Resonance: A Sociology of Our Relationship to the World*[1] is the long-awaited follow-up to his groundbreaking studies of modern social acceleration and its consequences – primarily, alienation. His thesis is that modern human beings have a warped relationship with the world – with nature, animals and other people – because we have turned them into resources, whose sole value is derived from the extent to which we can transform them into something that benefits us. In other words, we have instrumentalized our relationship with the world, and this quickly leads to the sad conclusion that we, too, have also become instruments, not only in the lives of others but also in our own lives. We need to optimize ourselves constantly in an attempt to keep up with the social acceleration promulgated by the rat race. It alienates us when we are turned into resources, like goods exchanged in a market to make a profit.

Rosa's new book on resonance attempts to present some kind of solution to this problem of alienation, some sort of cure. He suggests that it lies in the resonance that he believes exists when we are in a 'responsive' relationship with the world – in other words, when we don't simply react mechanically to what's going on around us but engage in meaningful ways in particular contexts. We experience resonance when we reply or respond to the world, and it responds to us. When things are not just dead objects with no meaning and history, when animals and the rest of nature are not just production units, and other people are not just human resources used to maximize profit.

Resonance is a metaphor from acoustics (the science of sound), and Rosa uses the example of two tuning forks, one of which is set off by the sound produced by the other. It's not just an echo, with the sound of one fork cast back unchanged from the other. Resonance entails several elements vibrating together and changing each other in the process. While this may sound a little abstract, Rosa proffers many examples of resonance in non-acoustic contexts, from sport and movement to food, sex and breathing. He believes that we can establish 'resonance relationships' horizontally (to other people), diagonally (to the world of objects) and vertically (to the cosmos as a whole). It is in relation to the vertical that I find his thinking relevant to my study of the possible meaning of religion in the modern world.

Rosa dedicates an entire chapter to religion, which he defines as follows: 'Religion can be understood as the idea, expressed through rites and practices, songs and stories, art and architecture, that this *something* is responsive, accommodating – and understanding.'[2] By italicising '*something*', he emphasizes that the world can be perceived not only as a series of dead and mute objects on to which we attempt to project meaning, but as something with which we may engage in some kind of conversation, and which is capable of responding to us. A good life is one in which we are in a 'conversational' relationship with the world. And that is precisely what a religious outlook can provide.

The twentieth-century philosopher Martin Buber was renowned for his writings on dialogue, particularly his distinction between relating to a 'Thou' and an 'It' (things). When we relate to something else as an 'It' – for example, another human being – we treat it as an object. We can reduce another human being to an 'It' if we see them as a kind of machine made of meat, but we can also reduce the world as a whole to a collection of 'Its', which is the opposite of resonance. Conversely, when we relate to the world as a whole in a way that allows it to speak to us, we are in resonance with it, and it becomes a 'Thou'.

Rosa writes that God is basically a term for the idea that the world is responsive to us. When we send our words or actions out into the world and listen to what happens, what we hear is not just our own echo but the world responding to us. The opposite to this is the view put forward by some existentialists, such as Albert Camus, that the world is absurd and ultimately meaningless. According to Jean-Paul Sartre, once we recognize that the world is dead and mute, we experience a profound sense of nausea. These atheist existentialists accepted the ultimate consequences of a scientific worldview in which meaning and value only stem from the

projections of free individuals. In short, meaning and value
don't exist until we decide to find them. According to them,
free will creates meaning, and then we project that meaning
on to an absurd world – like light on an empty cinema
screen. Anything significant, meaningful or sacred is only so
because we have decided it is. This is the basis of existential-
ism and has, in many ways, become the prevailing worldview
of the modern human being.

My copy of Rosa's book is full of underlining and notes on
the pages where he discusses religion and God in the light of
the concept of resonance. He also refers to William James,
who believed that religion was the term used to describe
humankind's 'total reaction upon life'. And that's exactly
what I'm looking for – an understanding of our relationship
to life that doesn't just reduce the world to silent, dead, cold,
mute objects that we are allowed to use as we deem fit, but
which instead sees the world as full of significant, conversational, warm, living phenomena. According to Rosa, seeking
this is a religious impulse. But, I wonder, is this the same as
saying that we can also be brought to *believe* that the world
is like this? It is one thing to wish it were the case; whether
I can believe it is another. Is the notion of God necessary in
order to find resonance with the world as a whole, or might
the same outcome be achieved through animism (faith in
a world of the soul) or polytheism (the belief in multiple
deities)?

The aforementioned Charles Taylor – himself a Catholic
– provides an exemplary description of what perception of
humankind and the world is linked to Rosa's concept of
resonance:

We live in a nature of deep time and unfathomable spaces,
from which we emerged. It is a universe which is in many
ways strange and alien, and certainly unfathomable. This
nourishes on the one hand a sense of kinship and filiation.
We belong to the earth; it is our home. This sensibility is a

powerful source of ecological consciousness. It also means
that we are led to think of ourselves as having a deep
nature, which we need to retrieve, or perhaps overcome;
something which we can find out how to do by examining
our dark genesis.[3]

We are part of a universe, a nature, not of our making, and
the world in which we live accommodates something we can
discover, and not simply choose or not as we see fit. Taylor
attaches great moral importance to this. He is deeply sceptical about the idea that it is possible to detach morality from
religion. The exclusive humanism mentioned earlier is not
enough because human beings stem from and participate in
a world that is not human. I will return to the link between
religion and morality later on.

6 February

To find out what religion really is, it might be worth considering whether, despite my modern, secular standpoint,
I *already* make use of a religious mindset – no matter how
implicitly. A few months ago, in my programme on Danish
radio, I talked to the religious scholar Anders Klostergaard
Petersen, who also works as an assistant minister in a church.
In other words, he combines a quite hardcore scientific perspective on religion, which he looks at from an evolutionary
perspective, with the act of ministering to a flock. He has
excellent knowledge of faith – and apparently a great faith in
knowledge! Among other things, he once wrote that *Homo
sapiens* 'developed religion to survive on the savannah, to
build the stable social structures needed. Contrary to popular
belief, humans are not very socially minded. The first people,
like the apes of today, lived in loose social communities that
regularly broke up. But we can't survive without the group,
so we had to develop a culture that supports communal
living.'[4] From this perspective, religion is a means of survival

because it creates unity in the flock. The historian Yuval Noah Harari – author of the bestseller *Sapiens* – advocates a similar concept. He believes that the human ability to create fictions such as God, Society or Coca-Cola (the brand – not the liquid) is absolutely crucial to our ability to work together in large numbers and on complex tasks.

What interests me most about this approach, however, is the distinction between faith and religion. In my mind, the two have always belonged together: you are religious if you have faith, and faith is something religious. In other words, religiosity is a specific state of mind characterized by faith. Not according to Petersen. He says religion is 'not synonymous with "faith", which came much later. Religion is a repository in which the collective stores its positive feelings, and in doing so affirms that it is a community.' Religion is historically very different from faith because religion is a term for the collective rituals and practices that – via emotions – bind people to the community and make larger societies possible. Faith only comes into play in recent centuries, especially with Protestantism and its individualistic – and perhaps even 'psychologized' – relationship with religion, in which it is the individual's experience of faith that is essential. A Protestant is redeemed not by deeds, but through faith. It sounds difficult because we can manage and control deeds to a certain extent, but faith is a different matter – like falling in love, as mentioned earlier. It is not something we can choose, which means that Protestants are, in a radical sense, in God's hands.

If this understanding of religion is valid, then I suppose that I *am* already religious, even though I wouldn't say that I have faith. Perhaps we're all religious – whether we have personal faith or not – at least as long as we live in and feel responsible for our communities? A more tangible example might help. At the moment, I'm conducting research into what we call the culture of grief – that is, the changing cultural conditions for grief as a basic human phenomenon.

As part of this work, I have discovered something that surely ought to be self-evident (and, therefore, paradoxically difficult to detect) – i.e. that many of our practices concerning the dead are difficult to explain in purely secular terms. For example, no matter how pigheadedly materialistic we are in a philosophical sense (i.e. we believe everything in the world can be explained exhaustively in physical/chemical terms), we still care about the wishes of the dead. We read the last will and testament of the deceased with interest and try to abide by it. We know the deceased wanted a particular hymn at the funeral, and we sing it. Nobody would dream of saying, 'Who cares what he wanted. He's dead now. Why bother?' But why not? The deceased *is* dead, so what does it matter to him?

The Swedish philosopher Hans Ruin furnishes us with one answer. He explains that we live *a life with the dead*. We have a form of intersubjectivity (i.e. contact with each other) that doesn't just pertain to the living but also extends to the dead.[5] We can actually *owe* the dead something – including fulfilling their wishes when feasible. They may be dead and unable to do anything about it, but ignoring their wishes *does* matter. Ruin also puts it another way: that our life, as a living being, is always a life *after someone*, as part of which we are responsible for the afterlife of the dead. The Danish theologian and philosopher K. E. Løgstrup's famous ethical demand stems from the fact that all interaction with other human beings involves holding some part of that person's life in our hands, which is why we should use that power for the good of the other. Applying this to Ruin's perspective on life with the dead, the ethical demand must also be extended to the dead: in a radical sense, we hold their *afterlife* in our hands as they no longer speak for themselves, and we owe it to them to use our power over them for their good, and not our own.

That we have a responsibility to the dead and owe them something also applies, of course, to their bodies. They may be lifeless corpses, but they can't yet be compared to fallen leaves or disposable waste. Again, even the most secular of people understand – at a very deep level – that we must treat the bodies of the dead with respect and dignity. All cultures have rituals and ceremonies for dealing with the dead. Why is that the case, given that the dead *are* dead? Well, perhaps because at this very basic level, we are all religious. We basically all have 'a total reaction upon life' (James' definition of religion), one example of which is a special reverence for the dead. We have a need to come together to mark the life and passing of the deceased, and rituals for treating their corpse in a dignified manner. These rituals, of course, take very different forms in different cultures, but they exist everywhere, in one form or another. In this sense, we are all religious – at least according to this definition of the term.

8 February

Yesterday, I had my first meeting about this book with my lovely editor. She likes it so far. Fortunately! She could see the relevance of the theme, as the question of religion has been coming up more and more often in recent times. She suggested that I foreground Christianity, and I agree. I don't want to be distracted by all sorts of spiritual, New Age concepts, as they would be too far removed from my personal and cultural standpoints. I would prefer to start from my own historical and cultural background. She left it up to me to decide whether I would look at other religions, such as Islam. But I don't think I should. It's already complicated enough dealing with religion in a framework with which I am relatively familiar. Quite simply, I'm not sufficiently well equipped to discuss the many differences between the monotheistic religions.

The editor raised an important point that I've also been thinking about. As a scientist interested in philosophy, my relationship with religion and faith is very much intellectual.

I immediately started delving into all sorts of academic literature and profound debates regarding the basic concepts linked to religion. And I will continue to do that because it is, after all, a sincere reflection of who I am, and I truly believe that there is something to be learned from the great thinkers of our day, such as Taylor and Rosa. But I must also remember that this isn't how most people feel. For most people, religion is more experiential. In other words, it is grounded in their experience of something sacred, be it God's presence, the joy of His Creation, etc. – what Rosa calls resonance. Of course, this dimension is not totally alien to me, and I have already described a deeply meaningful and personal experience of my own, but this is definitely a fundamental issue that I must remember to address. I won't be withdrawing to a monastery to do so, though. That would be too contrived and maybe even trivialize my study of religion.

10 February

I have spent the last few days looking for signs of religious thinking in my own writing. Why? Well, I suspect that my personal and research interest in meaning and values (about which I have written a great deal) reflects much the same impulse that is now driving me to look at religion. I stumbled across a chapter I wrote fourteen years ago for a book about religion in modern working life.[6] In it, I argue that, in some contexts, psychology acts as a kind of religion for people in modern Western society.

I began the chapter with a fresh (I thought!) analysis of the difference between Karl Marx's day and the industrial society of the nineteenth century and the present. Marx famously regarded religion as the 'opium of the masses'! In other words, his idea of God and cosmic justice was of something used to pacify the workers so that they would put up with oppression and wage slavery in an exploitative and alienating capitalist system. But today – I asserted – religion is perhaps more the Ritalin of the masses! Ritalin is a type of amphetamine mainly used to alleviate the symptoms of ADHD. It can regulate sleep, enhance a sense of wellbeing and self-confidence, focus and channel our ability to act, sharpen the senses and increase brain activity. According to the classical sociologist Max Weber, the Protestant religion made us focused, purposeful and disciplined. Today, it is rarely Protestantism that fulfils this function, as people turn more to meditation, spirituality and self-development. Religion no longer *oppresses* us as a kind of opium, but *develops us*, makes us productive, innovative and hard-working – just like Ritalin.

But what *is* religion then, given that it can be considered comparable to both opium and Ritalin? My old chapter offered an answer to this, too. Armin W. Geertz defined religion as a 'cultural system and a social institution that governs and promotes ideal interpretations of existence and ideal praxis with reference to postulated transempirical powers or beings'.[7] This sounds a bit technical, so let's boil it down to its three basic elements: (1) a *practical* element (a cultural system in which religion is something you *do*); (2) a *normative* element (what you *ought* to do); and (3) a *metaphysical* element (in the form of 'transempirical' powers or beings that affect the course of the world).

I argued that many psychological concepts are transempirical in that they refer to something that cannot be observed with the senses – consider, for example, a phenomenon such as the Self, understood as an intrinsic inner essence. I also claimed that psychologists had become a new priesthood, having simply replaced confession and tending to the soul with psychotherapy; grace and salvation with self-realization; and God with the Self. In this way, psychology has become a religion – or at least an alternative to religion – but one that supports the individual's quest for self-realization rather than fostering commitment to a deeper dimension of life.

In many ways, I think this analysis still holds, as society has become even more psychologized. But what is also interesting in this context is that Geertz includes the central element that most people probably see as being at the heart of religion – namely, the idea of a power that transcends the ordinary world of the human senses. Without that element, there is a risk of the idea being diluted since all cultural practices that incorporate rituals and are based on ideals could be considered religious phenomena.

24 February

Reading my notes for this month, it's clear that I have been juxtaposing two approaches to religion: one that emphasizes its function as one of the pillars of society, and another one that also invokes powers that transcend those of the human world. Other scientific discussions of religion have thrown up similar distinctions – very often between the *systemic* (religion as a system of practices) and the *experiential* (religion as a specific kind of experience). The sociologist of religion Bryan Turner defines religion *both* as 'a system of symbols and values which, through their emotional impact, not only bind people together into a sacred community but induce a normative and altruistic commitment to collective ends' *and* simply as 'the experience of the holy'.[8]

The first definition is collectivist and stresses culturally developed ways of establishing social bonds. The second is more individualistic and stresses personal experience. The former is usually associated with Émile Durkheim, one of the founders of sociology in the nineteenth century, who perceived religion as a kind of social glue that binds a given community. The latter can be linked to William James, who was more interested in how the individual is influenced by religious experiences. Turner himself underlines that this distinction is not as interesting from a scientific perspective. In his sociological view, he says that, on the one hand, the individual's experience is always socially conditioned because religious experience stems from the collective, while, on the other, the collective can be said to consist of individuals. Coming from a scientific tradition (cultural psychology) that seeks to break down excessively sharp divisions between practice and person, culture and actor, I understand this argument. Having said that, I also think that it undermines the possibility of religious experiences that are not directly supported by rituals or collective practices. All experiences are, of course, specific to a time and place, but my Sardinian experience, for example – or the countless testimonies from others who have had similar experiences – suggest that religious experiences can also strike almost without warning. I think that there are probably universal human experiences of a 'cosmic nature' (for want of a better term) that can be deciphered as religious. However, our interpretation of them, the importance they are afforded, and the techniques and rituals used to try and conjure them up vary significantly from culture to culture.

A very similar view is found in the excellent *Religion in Human Evolution* by the late sociologist Robert N. Bellah.[9] Published when the author was 84, the book outlines a theory of religion, but also describes the evolution of religiosity from the early Stone Age to the 'Axial' epoch (around the time of Buddha, Confucius and the pre-Socratic philosophers). Bellah combines a broad knowledge of biology and evolution with deep insight into the cultural and social sciences, and also manages to write scientifically about religion from a Christian (Episcopalian) perspective. Early in the book, he endorses a variant of the cultural scientist Clifford Geertz' definition of religion (a different Geertz from the Armin mentioned above): 'A religion is a system of symbols which acts to establish powerful, pervasive and long-lasting moods in men by formulating conceptions of a general order of existence.'[10]

By referencing Geertz, Bellah takes into account both sides of the coin. Religion is both a system of symbols and acts (e.g. rituals) *and* something rooted in our experiences (e.g. feelings of reverence). If religion were *only* external, it would not make sense to the individual. If it were *only* internal, it would not have the social significance that we see everywhere in the world and throughout history. Religion, therefore, consists of symbolic forms and actions that allow people to interpret the ultimate questions in life. This sounds like a workable definition.

26 February

This month, I have explored definitions of religion and faith. I hope this work will prove to be a helpful preparatory exercise for my studies during the rest of the year. First, I made a distinction between the concepts of religion and faith. *Believing in something* – as a concrete state of mind or a mental process – is different from being religious in the sense of taking part in collective activities that utilize rituals to foster emotional unity and sustain communities. Faith is the attitude *of the individual*, while religion is a *social* practice. We can, therefore, at least in principle, be religious without being a believer, and we may also be a believer without being religious (although the latter is more difficult to imagine since it would require an isolated individual, outside of their society and community, with their own unique idea of faith).

One problem with our modern, secularized perspective is that we have become accustomed to assuming that faith is the path to salvation – at least in the Protestant world – and therefore in itself a sign of religiosity. When faith becomes just one option among many, what then are the arguments in favour of believing? It is not enough just to participate in religious practices. We also have to have faith. That is why 'apologetic' texts are still written defending the legitimacy – perhaps even necessity – of faith.

March

Is there a link between ethics and faith?

1 March

In recent years, I have been studying the key values and issues in life (I call them *standpoints*) in an attempt to develop an analysis that doesn't just see them as originating solely from the individual. I have defended a moral realism in which it is not up to the sovereign individual to define what is true and good. To use religious terminology, the crux of this point of view is that human beings are not God. My recurring argument has been that, like it or not, simply being one human being among many means that we have obligations to one another. I have also sought to convey the idea that, even if it may at first appear limiting, this idea is actually quite liberating – not everything is up to me, but there are things in life that I should try to do as well as possible. I think it is an edifying insight.

Given these reflections, it is no surprise that people have asked me questions like: Where do these obligations and standpoints stem from? Who came up with them? Does my concept of human ethics not assume faith in a divine higher power? What is the relationship between living a moral life and faith? Between ethics and religion?

Hopefully, this book attests to the fact that I do not seek to declare religion invalid. The fact that my view of life has not made mention of the divine to date in no way means that I have actively avoided it. Until now, I have maintained Søren Kierkegaard's distinction between ethics and religion, and stuck to studying ethics. This is because, in my opinion, letting religion dictate to or influence ethics is highly problematic.

In *Fear and Trepidation*, written under the pseudonym Johannes de Silentio, Kierkegaard asked his famous question: 'Is there a teleological suspension of the ethical?' In other words, are there higher purposes in life than ethical ones? Consider, for example, when God orders Abraham to sacrifice his son Isaac and places the religious dimension above any ethical obligation to his child. For Kierkegaard, the answer is obvious: Yes. But this means that we end up being seduced into a kind of fundamentalism. According to Kierkegaard, there are situations in which a higher authority requires that we sacrifice the ethical dimension in our human interactions. I remember how shocked I was when I first read this and grasped the deep religious fundamentalism my famous compatriot was advocating. He may not take the Bible literally, but the assertion that religion can supersede ethics in certain situations makes Kierkegaard a fundamentalist, in my opinion.

These days, if anybody claimed to hear God's voice ordering them to kill a child, we would – rightly, I think – consider it a symptom of psychosis and have them sectioned. In situations like that, we do *not* – thankfully – allow anything to be put before ethics, and Kierkegaard's seeming approval of it has often, and with good reason, been criticized. The philosopher and ethicist Emmanuel Levinas criticized what he saw as Kierkegaard's 'violence'. For Levinas, allowing religious commandments to take precedence over ethics is a form of violence and must never be tolerated. I agree. I've spent hours discussing it with Kierkegaard-savvy friends, who have defended his reading of the story of Abraham, but I remain unconvinced. Putting religion before ethics can, in radical cases, turn into terror, of which we have seen far too many examples in recent years. I might add that I am not positing it as an argument against religion per se that certain people are violent in its name. What I *would* say, however, is that religion operates in a different sphere from ethics and that we must be cautious not to confuse the two. Doing so leaves us vulnerable to violence.

More than a century ago, the famous philosophers Ludwig Wittgenstein and Moritz Schlick debated whether that which is good is good because it is what God wants – or whether God wants that which is good because it is good. I almost always agree with Wittgenstein, but not this time. He adopted the former stance, which implies that it would be good to kill your child if God willed it. I agree with the latter: if there is a God, He would want that which is good because it is good. In this way, 'good', in the words of the philosopher Iris Murdoch, is a 'sovereign concept' that requires no external validation, because it justifies itself.[1] We might even interpret the biblical story of the Creation as bearing the same message: God first lets there be light, after which 'And God saw that the light, that it was good, and God divided the light from the darkness.' God *saw* that it was good. He did not *choose* it to be good. He probably wanted there to be light precisely because it *was* good. He wants that which is good *because* it's good.

This reflects my thinking in recent years: that we can and should understand ethics and morality without recourse to religion. This is not to say that religion doesn't matter, just that it isn't the same as ethics. If good exists, God wants it. Otherwise, he wouldn't be God, would he? And if God doesn't exist, the ethical demand to look after other people *still* pertains.

The debate about religion and ethics is not confined solely to Christianity. Plato posed the question of God and the good in the dialogue *Euthyphro*, around 375 BCE.[2] As usual, Socrates is the protagonist. He is on his way to Athens to hear the charges against him – introducing new gods, and not believing in the city state's ancient deities. We know that he will ultimately be sentenced to death, but he doesn't know it yet. On the way, he meets his old friend Euthyphro, and they talk. The conversation is mainly about the nature of 'piety' and whether belief in the gods is fundamental to morality. Socrates' question to his friend is: is the pious loved by the gods because it is pious, or is it pious because it is loved by the gods?[3]

This is the ancient equivalent of the debate between Wittgenstein and Schlick: is the good good because God / the gods want it, or do God / the gods want it because it's good?

Socrates and Euthyphro discuss the idea that, if the gods approve of an action, then it is either random and completely without reason, in which case its value derives solely from its divine endorsement; or, the gods approve of the action for a reason, which must mean that the act has independent moral value, even without the mediation of the gods. If the former is the case, then what is good is, in fact, a completely arbitrary reflection of the will of the gods, who in principle might have declared the opposite to be good. This seems somewhat unsatisfactory to us mere mortals who are expected to try to live in accordance with the good (whatever it may be). Why should we base our lives on something so arbitrary? But if the latter is the case, then the gods are superfluous to our definition of what is good, because it is good per se, gods or no gods. Ergo, Socrates thought we should differentiate between religion and ethics, as they are two completely different things. Given that Socrates demonstrated 2,500 years ago that we don't need gods to understand what is good and right, it is easy to see why a profoundly religious society would condemn him to death. However, there is also a third possibility worth exploring: that God, the gods or the divine are simply terms we apply to 'the power of good' (or whatever we want to call it). If that is the case, it makes little sense to ask whether God wants that which is good because God *is* that which is good; or whether that which is good is good because God wants it because God *is* good. We might say that the divine is nothing more than goodness. I put 'the power of good' in quotation marks because, at first glance, it sounds like the most banal form of shallow spirituality. This may not be a position that is easy to express in a rational and accessible way in the modern world, but I will give it a go tomorrow because I think I'm on to something important here . . .

2 March

One of the philosophers who has meant the most to me and who has written about the relationship between God and the good is Iris Murdoch, whom I mentioned in passing yesterday.[4] She was one of the few twentieth-century philosophers to hark all the way back to Plato, finding in him a basic recognition of the reality outside of the self and a celebration of the power of good – or, as she called it, 'the sovereignty of good'.[5] For Murdoch, good is a sovereign concept, which means that – as for all other moral concepts – we can ask, 'But is it really good?' Yes, we ought to be loyal because loyalty is a virtue. But is it *always* good to be loyal? This is a meaningful question because the demand for loyalty may conflict with, for example, a value such as universal justice. Similarly, yes, we should speak the truth, but is the truth *always* good? That question, too, is meaningful because it is conceivable that, in many situations, there could be a moral imperative to lie. When we define the good as something specific – an x – we must necessarily add that we mean a *good* x. It is not meaningful, on the other hand, to ask whether the good (thing) is good – because it is so purely by definition. According to Murdoch, then, there is necessarily something inherently undefinable and partially incomprehensible about that which is good. Good has a reality that exceeds our limited comprehension. And yet we are able to recognize the good when we become aware of it in specific situations. In both her philosophy and her literature (many may know her primarily as a novelist), Murdoch was particularly adept at describing the good. Many of us are probably familiar with the experience of being moved by the gratuitous goodness of strangers. In a world where people are often preoccupied with their own concerns, sudden acts of selflessness can brighten our day and be deeply moving. Murdoch asserts that this is precisely what Plato was trying to illustrate in his famous Allegory of the Cave – that good exists outside us as some kind of authority. In the allegory, Plato imagines people trapped in a cave, where the only reality they know consists of shadows cast on the wall by a fire. The shapes on the cave wall are merely a crude facsimile of the world outside the cave, which is illuminated and given life by the scorching sunlight. The sun is a symbol of the good that nobody completely understands. It cannot be observed directly, but that does not mean, either for Plato or for Murdoch, that it is an illusion. It is the same with the good. Murdoch was eminently effective at explaining how we can experience the good as something that exists both prior to and independently of the will of the individual. I cannot just decide or choose what counts as good. Rather, there is a kind of truth to it that transcends my subjective perspective. Consider, for example, the story of the Good Samaritan from the Gospel according to Saint Luke – perhaps the most famous of all Jesus' parables. It becomes evident to the Jewish person to whom Jesus is talking that the Samaritan's actions are good (even though, at that time, the Jews looked down on the Samaritans), simply because he helps a fellow human being in need. Most people who hear the story today understand that the Samaritan is doing something good. In the situation, he embodies what Løgstrup called 'the ethical demand': to use our power over fellow human beings in any given situation for the good of the other, not for our own good.[6] This demand arises from the situation itself – it is, in Løgstrup's words, 'unspoken' because it does not arise from an agreement, a contract based on reciprocity or because the other expresses a desire for help. It is the very *fact* that this power to help the other is inescapable that constitutes the demand placed on us. To help is our human calling.

Reflecting on the concepts of God and the good, Murdoch defines God as 'a single perfect, transcendent, non-representable and necessarily real object of attention'.[7] While this sounds somewhat technical, I think it corresponds quite closely to a standard theological view: that God is something outside the Self – something perfect, and which cannot be fully comprehended by the human mind (it is 'non-representable'), yet to which we can nevertheless direct our attention. Murdoch thinks that moral philosophy ought to take an interest in this concept of God, and posits that it is realized in the idea of the good. The good is something outside the Self, which we cannot fully comprehend, yet to which we must nevertheless direct our attention.

Murdoch's concept of love (again, derived from Plato) is also relevant in this context. In her eyes, love is a form of attention directed away from the Self and out towards the world. For this reason, we cannot, by definition, love ourselves.[8] Goodness, she writes, is the 'ability to perceive what is true, which is automatically at the same time a suppression of self'.[9] When we meet a person in dire need, our own needs are of no consequence. The situation requires that we transcend our vanity, greed and self-absorption in order to arrive at a true understanding of how we ought to act. Love is the ability to *look beyond* the Self to recognize what is out there and what we ought to do. Love liberates the Self from its egotistical fantasies. Murdoch is well aware that this sounds old-fashioned and asks herself whether she really believes that good exists as an idea or force 'out there'. She concludes that it does not, at least not in quite the same way as people used to believe in a personal God (the bearded old man in Heaven). However, she still believes that good manifests itself in our experiences and that we have a need for concepts and metaphors that allow us to recognize the characteristics of the good whenever we encounter them.[10]

I find Murdoch's essay on God and the good deeply inspiring. She argues that the two concepts are closely aligned – or at least that the essence of what we mean when we refer to God is something like true goodness, the moral imperative, that which makes demands of us. This conceptualization also reflects the traditional monotheistic definition of God as omnibenevolent, omnipotent and omniscient. From this perspective, religion is about how we as human beings learn to direct ourselves outward towards the world and engage with reality to the fullest extent possible, rather than just being attentive to our own subjective wishes. If this concept of God is valid, it is a matter of seeing the world *more* objectively, not *less* so. From this perspective, religion is not about wrapping people up in illusions, but about freeing them from self-absorption so that they may see the world more clearly. A religion that fails to do this is not worth following.

What role can faith play in this perspective? It is about the world being worth loving, even if terrible things happen; helping those in need, even if there is no quid pro quo; life being worth living even though it will end one day. The question, then, is whether such a concept of God can satisfy believers' wishes. How can the idea of 'the good' instil hope? How can it relieve deep pain or provide consolation after a tragic loss? Do we need to take seriously the fact that many people have a need for more tangible versions of faith – like, for example, a man with a beard in Heaven, resurrection and eternal life? Or should we conclude that the hope of eternal life may itself be a form of self-absorption, in which we cannot tolerate the idea that our tiny little egos won't exist forever? My first instinct is to concur with the latter. Perhaps this also explains why the old religious commandment 'Thou shalt believe in God!' has now been supplanted by the psychological commandment 'Thou shalt believe in thyself!' Many of us have become so self-indulgent that we can't imagine the world without ourselves in it. According to Murdoch, this can be an impediment to the love of the world that will supposedly make us do good deeds. Might we today proclaim, 'Thou shalt believe in good!' as a relevant religious commandment? I would like to think so.

13 March

The country has gone into lockdown due to the coronavirus. That in itself warrants some religious contemplation. Why do things that harm and kill people, like this virus, exist if God is so benevolent and omnipotent? This is the classic theodicy problem, which has been debated throughout the history of Christianity. It is particularly pertinent when it comes to the relationship between religion and ethics.

I have learnt about a surprising perspective on this whole issue known as the theology of the 'weak God'.[11] I ask the reader to forgive me in advance because what I am about to attempt to convey is, I think, quite difficult to understand. But let's persevere. I've certainly found it worthwhile.

The great monotheistic religions – based on holy books such as the Bible and the Quran – appear to present God as big and strong. He is, in effect, a kind of Superman because he can help us, intervene in the world and maybe even perform miracles. In principle, he can also punish us (if we're unlucky) or our enemies (if he's on our side). The theology of the 'weak God' rejects this view, arguing that God is weak, has no superpowers (indeed, barely any power at all) and, in a sense, doesn't exist at all. How can such ideas be considered religious or theological? Who thinks like that? John D. Caputo, for one – a softly spoken American philosopher by whom I have been quite enthralled of late.

One of Caputo's books, which is about not only God's weakness, but also his folly, opens with Paul's First Epistle to the Corinthians:

Where is the wise? where is the scribe? where is the disputer
of this world? hath not God made foolish the wisdom of
this world?

For after that in the wisdom of God the world by
wisdom knew not God, it pleased God by the foolishness
of the preaching to save them that believe.

For the Jews require a sign, and the Greeks seek after
wisdom:

But we preach Christ crucified, unto the Jews a stumbling block, and unto the Greeks foolishness;

But unto them which are called, both Jews and Greeks,
Christ the power of God, and the wisdom of God.

Because the foolishness of God is wiser than men, and
the weakness of God is stronger than men.[12]

Paul writes like an early social anthropologist studying cultures and peoples: the Jews demand signs; the Greeks seek
wisdom. It is in the nature of both that they seek evidence.
Here, of course, he is thinking of the Greek philosophers
like Socrates, Plato and Aristotle, who loved wisdom (which
is what philosophy means in Greek), and the Jewish people
of the day who apparently saw signs in everything. But
Christianity speaks of a God who became human and was
even weak enough to die a mortal death on the Cross. God
allowed himself to be born as a human being and then be
humiliated, tortured and executed. A God who does this
must be weak, yet Paul adds that 'the weakness of God is
stronger than men'! What does that mean?

From this starting point, Caputo develops a whole train
of thought about weakness. In his opinion, it is superstition
and wishful thinking to imagine God as the supreme being,
as some kind of magical entity with superpowers. However,
even though it may be classified as wishful thinking – because
it may be comforting to believe in a strong force that con-
trols everything – Caputo argues that it is still undesirable.
His reasoning is that, if God really were to turn out to be

a supreme being, then the Kingdom of God would be an impossibility! What does he mean by this? For Caputo, God is the best concept we have for *the unconditional* – it refers to the existence of something that places demands on us without imposing conditions. Just like Løgstrup's ethical demand: like the Good Samaritan, we should help those in need. But why? To receive something in return, to appear heroic or good, to lower our blood pressure and reduce our stress levels, or maybe even to go to Heaven? No, because answers like that make the demand conditional, in effect saying that we are only obliged to help the other *if* there's something in it for us – which negates the unconditional aspect of the concept. When we make the right course of action conditional on a quid pro quo, we prevent ourselves from understanding the unconditional.

It is not just the ethical demand in the encounter with others that has this peculiar, unconditional quality – it also applies to forgiveness (which is not forgiveness if it is only proffered when it benefits the giver), love (which is not love if it is only given to be loved in return) and hospitality (which is not hospitable if it requires the guest to return the favour), etc. I call all such phenomena *standpoints* because it is worth standing firm on them in a world in a state of constant flux.

For Caputo, theology is simply the best tool for thinking about the unconditional. This is where it all becomes a bit tricky because, in his weak theology, the unconditional (i.e. God) doesn't *exist*. At least not in the way that we usually say something exists. I can see my hands typing on the keyboard in front of me – they exist. I can hear my children in the living room next door (they have been sent home from school because of the pandemic) – they exist. The books on my bookcase exist. The cars driving past on the road outside exist. But we can't say in the same way that the unconditional *exists*. Instead, to use Caputo's term, it *insists*. The unconditional does not exist as an active, quantifiable force in the universe, like gravity or magnetism. To believe that would be superstition. It would entail turning religion into a primitive pseudoscience about an invisible super-powered being. The unconditional, on the other hand, *insists*, in the form of an opportunity to do the right thing, even when it is more convenient not to do so. Speak the truth. Keep your promises. Love thy neighbour. But why? Because there is an almighty God who commands it and will punish you if you don't? No. To do that is to make the unconditional conditional on something else – specifically, on the supreme being, in which case it is no longer unconditional. If the good is conditioned by God's existence, it is not unconditionally good. If my motivation to comply with the demand that I help the other is solely due to my fear of God, then my action is, in effect, a kind of settling of accounts (the law of karma, or whatever we want to call it). It is not directed at the unconditional demand itself. In that case, what drives us to do good is ultimately little more than fear or vanity – both of which are conditional.

It is crucial that there is no omnipotent force behind the unconditional. If there were, the unconditional would be conditional, as it would be predicated on the existence of this force. Rather, what drives us is the calling or insistence of the unconditional. The idea of weakness stems from this conception of God as a force without strength, an insistence without existence, a power without the power to reward or punish. According to Caputo, this is precisely Christianity's radical insight, given at the moment of Jesus' death. He goes on to describe it as a kind of folly, as Paul also wrote about in his Epistle to the Corinthians: the folly of God, who is wiser than us. God's folly is that he does not exist, he insists – even insisting on something that, in the context of a something-for-something logic, seems baffling, and yet we must live by it. It is generally believed that it's better to fight back, take revenge, think opportunistically, only surround ourselves with people who give energy rather than sap it from us. We only do what we're paid to do, right? In that light, it is folly to turn the other cheek, to forgive, to love unconditionally. Why do that? Jesus even demanded that we love our enemies. But it's simply not worth it if there is no reward.

According to Caputo, as soon as we ask 'why?' we have departed the Kingdom of God, which is precisely where we are *not* guided by a strong hand, where we listen for weak insistence. Acting mercifully will not earn us admission to the Kingdom of God because it is not something we *can* earn, because that would make it conditional ('we can only enter *if*. . .'). Simply put, the unselfish act *is* the Kingdom of God.[13] In Caputo's theology of weakness, there is no Heaven in the hereafter, no divine power, no Yahweh punishing and rewarding, yet we can hear the quiet calls from 'the nothings and the nobodies of the world'. He sees Jesus as the embodiment of these calls – an expression of solidarity with those who are crushed by the world, who need help without being able to give anything in return.[14] In some ways, helping them, too, is a form of folly – a break with all economic, mercantile, opportunistic and Darwinian logic. To give voice to the unconditional seems like a form of ethical madness in a world obsessed with balancing the books and received wisdom.

(Phew! I hope you're still with me! I've spent a lot of time trying to grasp this line of thinking myself and am still mulling it over.)

The consequence of God not existing (but insisting) is that it removes metaphysics from religion. You can't draw maps of Heaven and Hell (which, by the way, are rarely mentioned in the Bible) because they are places that don't exist, just as God is not a figure that exists. Therein lies the crux of the weak God: if an omnipotent deity were suddenly to exist, then all that is unconditional – all that is precious in life – would become transactional, part of a bartering system based on human deeds, rewards and punishments. Paradoxically, this would destroy the Kingdom of God.[15]

Imagine how much time we would have to set aside for set-tling our accounts with this almighty overlord! The Kingdom of God is only possible precisely because of God's weakness, because he died and became conspicuous by his absence. But what about the religious texts that mention angels and trumpets, miracles and burning bushes? One approach is to think of them as ancient poetry, to be read symbolically but not literally. This doesn't mean the texts aren't true – just that their value is not scientifically quantifiable. I will return to this later when I throw myself into the Bible.

It is not only ingenious theologians such as Caputo who advocate this paradoxical view of the Kingdom of God. In a lengthy account of both his own faith and that of the Apostle Paul, the French writer Emmanuel Carrère com-pares the notion of the Kingdom of God with ideas from Eastern religions, and concludes: 'An Indian sage speaks of "samsara" and "nirvana". "Samsara" is the world of change, desire and suffering in which we live. "Nirvana" is the one to which the enlightened gain access: deliverance, beatitude. But, the sage says, "those who differentiate between samsara and nirvana are in samsara. Those who no longer do are in nirvana."'[16]

I think it's the same with the Kingdom of God. It exists when we love unconditionally, come to the rescue or forgive without ulterior motive. It also exists when we ourselves are loved, rescued or forgiven. From this perspective, faith in God has roughly the same structure as forgiveness. As the French philosopher Jacques Derrida wrote in his famous analysis of the phenomenon, we can only forgive the unforgivable – otherwise, there would be nothing to forgive. In the same way, we can only believe the unbelievable. If God walked among us, it would not make sense to believe in him. After all, everyone would be able to see that this superhuman being who knew everything and could perform miracles was God. In the comedy film *Bruce Almighty*, the main character, played by Jim Carrey, becomes God for a week – and quickly finds out what a tough gig it is! It is impossible to believe in such a God. For faith to have meaning, God had to die. When we sincerely forgive someone – not for gain, but because we are bestowing the gift of forgiveness upon them – we implicitly express belief in the good. We are showing faith in God and the Kingdom of God, as embodied by the weak God who insists by his absence. This is ethically irrational and perhaps, therefore, reflects a religious interpretation of the world.

16 March

My examination of the relationship between ethics and religion has covered a lot of ground. I began by arguing that there is a difference between the two: that we ought not to use religion to justify our ethics because that way fundamentalism lies (for example, if we say, 'You must do what God commands, whatever it is, just because he says so!'). Given everyday conceptions of religion and the idea of God as a super-being, I still think that it makes sense to keep the two separate. However, if God is *not* a super-being, but an expression of the unconditional ethical demand, then the situation is different. In that case, religion's language for the unreserved, the unconditional, is suddenly the best – perhaps the only – language we can use to grasp how demands can insist – call on us – unconditionally, without the need for a superpower behind them keeping track of whether we are listening and behaving correctly.

In a certain sense, therefore, ethics only become possible with the death of God, when he stops existing and starts insisting. Only then can the unconditional begin to make demands of us. Friedrich Nietzsche notoriously declared that God is dead – a statement almost everyone will recognize. Less well known, however, is the addendum to this remark in his 1882 book *The Gay Science*: 'And we killed him!'[17]

Only that which once lived can die. As such, we might say that Nietzsche's statement implies that God once lived – at least as an idea of an actually existing metaphysical force in the world, something people could worship and pray to in the hope that rain would fall on the fields, or that eternal salvation might await them in the hereafter. However, modern humans, with their science and what Weber calls 'disenchantment', have killed this notion of God. The strong God is dead. Is that not a tragedy? No, because if the weak God is credible, then the death of God – the idea that he no longer exists – is faith's big opportunity. Only in his absence are we able to hear the weak calling of the unconditional and recognize that, as Caputo puts it, the Kingdom of God 'calls for a form of life that is mad about justice and forgiveness, come what may, even unto death'.[18]

I accept that these ideas about the weak God may sound strange. They go against much of what we have been told for millennia in a culture that is essentially based on two pillars: Greek philosophy and Christianity. As fond as I am of Greek philosophy – whose importance to European civilization is difficult to exaggerate – I must admit that Christianity raises important issues that Greek philosophy does not. Greek culture was born of ideals of honour and greatness. It was primarily about behaving in so noble a manner that you would be remembered and thereby achieve a form of immortality. The Greeks were terrified of being forgotten. Many of their myths are about the value of dying young and leaving an honourable legacy. It is not that these aspects of Greek thinking are worthless, but the problem is that they only celebrate that which is strong and honourable in life. For the ancient Greeks, men had value by virtue of their glorious deeds. Life was a struggle to realize the human potential for greatness, courage and other virtues. But what about those who aren't good or brave?

What about the humble, the excluded or the simply mediocre? After all, most of us belong to these categories, and, as such, we are overlooked in Greek thinking. Christianity's radical message, on the other hand, is that the right to enter the Kingdom of God is not something we can earn. All people have value – not because they perform great, heroic deeds, but simply because they are human beings. Jesus showed this by spending time with tax collectors and prostitutes and calling himself the Son of God, even though he was mocked, tortured and finally killed. On the Cross, Jesus is said to have shouted, 'My God, my God, why have you forsaken me?' – a mysterious and desperate outburst that can be understood in numerous ways. However, seen in the context of the weak God, it makes sense that Jesus would bid a despairing farewell to the idea of the powerful force that intervenes from above and has everything under control. When (the idea of) the strong force leaves us, we are left with nothing but a weak insistence on helping each other as much as possible. The unconditional task only becomes apparent when the strong God abandons us.

At any rate, to the Greeks, Jesus' radical idea of the unconditional value of all human beings (regardless of status or achievements) would have seemed most alien. 'For the Jews require a sign, and the Greeks seek after wisdom', as Paul wrote, 'But we preach Christ crucified, unto the Jews a stumbling block, and unto the Greeks foolishness.' I must admit that I have never fully understood this until now. Jesus' radicalism, which may even be construed as *folly*, lies in the fact that what religions and philosophies, both then and now, have highlighted as the strong (the super-force from on high) is, in fact, the weakest, most pitiable thing imaginable: a person in great torment in his hour of execution, who surrounded himself with the dregs of society because he insisted that their lives have value, too. Not bad for a carpenter's son 2,000 years ago.

The question is whether the idea remains as radical today as it was for the Greeks and pagans in Jesus' time. In modern society, we like to quantify people's value through tests, rankings, points and contributions to GDP. We measure, weigh and evaluate everything that is unconditional and, in doing so, make it conditional, based on its performance on different scales and parameters. I digress, admittedly, but I don't think that Jesus would have been a great fan of New Public Management. When you look at the work of the Christian churches over the centuries, it is also striking how far they have strayed from focusing on the unconditional. There have been missions, wars, fortunes amassed and 'witches' burnt at the stake – all in the name of Jesus, despite his unconditional care for the weak. It is not easy to reconcile the history of Christianity with the story of Jesus.

17 March

Reviewing what I have written in the last few days, I think I am gradually inching my way towards an understanding of Christianity and Jesus.

Many theologians will strongly disagree. My guess is that the idea of a weak God is a minority position in theology. Nonetheless, it strikes me as highly credible – in the real sense of the word that it is *worth believing* – especially for someone like me, who wants to explore the possibility of a faith capable of existing in harmony with what modern natural science teaches us. In fact, I think it is worth believing in this harmony, even if you believe there is nothing more between heaven and earth than there seems. The question is whether this weak conception of God and faith can be reconciled with organized religion, religious communities and ecclesiastical traditions. Can it respond to people's requests for comfort and substantiate their hopes of meeting loved ones again in an afterlife? Does it have anything to say to those seeking a more spiritual or experiential dimension to religion? While it is not my primary mission to enquire into such matters, I am aware that it is precisely the spiritual dimension that motivates many people to embark on a religious quest, so it is, of course, a relevant question to ask.

April

Does faith work?

1 April

I've been looking forward to April for months. We had a family holiday booked in Rome, with a hotel just behind St Peter's Basilica. I'd even booked tickets to see the Sistine Chapel, just before the Vatican gets mobbed during Easter. The Chapel is home to one of the world's most famous works of art, Michelangelo's early sixteenth-century ceiling frescoes depicting the Creation of Adam – the world-famous image in which God and Adam almost touch fingers.

I find the Catholic Church's grandeur and ceremonies fascinating. Although I do wonder what the humble Jesus would have made of the scale and opulence of it all. When I embarked on this study of religion and faith, I imagined Easter as a time I might feel the pull of religion in one of the world's great religious epicentres. Unfortunately, Italy has since become the epicentre of the COVID-19 pandemic as well, claiming thousands of lives as I write and plunging the nation into a state of crisis.

We're not going to Rome, of course. Not making the pilgrimage I had envisaged. There will be no great – possibly religious – experiences in St Peter's Square or the Sistine Chapel. In fact, like many Danes, I have to work at home at the moment, and I'm not allowed to travel and meet other people. This month, I will concentrate instead on whether faith works. That may sound like a funny way of putting it. What, exactly, does 'works' mean? It is a fairly common argument that the importance of faith should be quantified in terms of its effects on our life – or afterlife. In general, we live in an age when people are deeply concerned with whether things work. Will our treatment, teaching, social interventions and political reforms have the desired effect? Are we getting value for money? We live in a cause-and-effect regime, in which we focus on whether something *works* rather than what something actually *is*. We think more about utility than being, more about performance than existence. I rounded off March by discovering that I had considerable sympathy for the idea of the weak God – that the value of faith does not lie in the wonderful things it brings for the believer. Instead, faith is about accessing a world here and now ('the Kingdom of God') in which phenomena such as trust, love, forgiveness and mercy are meaningful, regardless of whether it is beneficial for the individual to live by them. We don't believe *in order to* achieve this or that; we believe simply because it is a true way of understanding the world.

The idea of the weak God, therefore, implies a firm rejection of attaching importance to the instrumental value of faith. But perhaps it is *too strong* a rejection. Is it not paradoxically the case – even in the weak theology introduced last month – that we must believe *in order to* recognize God's insistence? Even here, doesn't faith have some kind of effect, in that it allows us to embrace the unconditional? What's the point of acquiring all sorts of academic knowledge about theology or ethics if it makes no difference in day-to-day life? If we are not aware of the suffering person's need, then, in a sense, there's something we're not doing right. Here too, surely, faith must lead to some kind of action? After all, if the Good Samaritan doesn't perform good deeds, he's just a Samaritan.

Last month, my thinking revolved around the unconditional as the focal point of faith. But we shouldn't forget that faith is part of ordinary life as well, and we also have family and work. We want to be healthy, active and happy, and usually strive to be decent people. What effect do faith and religion have on these factors? It's difficult – if not impossible – to purge religion completely of such instrumental functions. As long as the field of religious studies has existed, sociologists and researchers have been interested in religion's role in society. This perspective, which sees religion as an instrument for nurturing solidarity and human communities, is definitely worth exploring.

The same applies to the more existential functions of religious belief. I have previously mentioned William James, the American psychologist who conducted in-depth studies of the religious experience more than a century ago. James belonged to the philosophical school known as pragmatism, which posits that an idea is true if it makes a positive difference to our lives. In the final analysis, therefore, truth is that which is conducive to a good and happy life. James himself believed that the depression he suffered in his youth stemmed from his adherence to a scientific worldview that had reduced him to a cog in a machine, lacking free will, trapped in a great game of cause and effect. He declared, unabashed, that his first free act was to believe in free will – which, by his own account, brought him out of his depression.

His claim is comparable to religious belief in a god. We will probably never be able to prove or disprove the existence of free will, any more than we can prove or disprove the existence of a god. But if faith in free will has beneficial effects – if it gives you a zest for life and allows you to live more freely – is that not sufficient reason to adopt it as a central pillar of the way you live? The prominent Enlightenment philosopher Immanuel Kant – who was by no means a pragmatist – had similar thoughts. Although we can't prove the existence of free will, a life *without* belief in the freedom of the will is inherently unfree and ultimately becomes absurd. For Kant, the fact that free will can manifest through *thought* was enough for it to have meaning in human life. We become freer simply by thinking that we are free. Likewise with God, belief in whom Kant terms a 'practical postulate'. We cannot prove God's existence positively, but we can believe that faith in God is a prerequisite for a moral life – in other words, faith has beneficial effects on our goodness and compassion.

Again, I think this idea is worthy of a closer look. Are religious people more likely to think that life is worth living and that the world is more or less meaningful? We often hear that this is the case and that this makes religious people happier than non-believers. But is it true? And what about other factors, such as health? Are religious people healthier? Do they live longer? Are they more likely to remain disease-free? Are they more altruistic and charitable? I would like to find out because the answers would indicate whether we should take the pragmatic effects of religion seriously. In the modern world, the emphasis is on whether things 'work'. Everyone keeps saying, 'we need to do what works'. So does faith work – and, if so, how?

2 April

In his best-known novel, *Atomised*, the author Michel Houellebecq asks: 'How could society function without religion? . . . It is difficult enough for an individual human being.'[1] Throughout the twentieth century, myriad voices expressed concern that secularization would lead to the collapse of society. I, myself, have been critical of how modern culture has replaced God with the Self (with a capital S). We have, in effect, developed a kind of religion of the Self. 'Believe in yourself!' we now intone, whereas in the past we would have been encouraged to believe in the creator. Today, we think of ourselves as the creator – at least of our own lives. Although the process is liberating in many ways, constant reaffirmation of belief in the Self comes at a price. With faith in the great power of self-creation comes great responsibility, as we know. It's not easy being God.

A society rooted in a traditional religion, such as Christianity, is usually based on a cultural order, with prevailing norms conveyed to the individual as a series of prohibitions. 'Thou shalt not' do this or that because it goes against the word of God, holy scripture or a Papal bull. However, secularization, and the individualization to which it has led in recent centuries, has gradually replaced the culture of prohibition with one of *command*. This is perhaps the biggest moral change between these two eras. Now, the prevailing norms are not formulated as things that we must *not* do, but as a requirement that individuals live their lives to the fullest, become the best version of themselves, accept new challenges. *Just Do It!* We all know the platitudes from advertising, self-help books and personal development courses. More than a century ago, Freud described the superego as the judgemental conscience – the part of us that said, 'No, you must not, even if you want to.' Now, we have a new superego, which doesn't say 'Suppress your desires.' It says, 'Do it *because* you want to.' The philosopher Slavoj Žižek[2] observes that we used to be duty-bound to give in order to get, but we now have a duty to enjoy ourselves. 'Enjoy!', we constantly remind each other. If you fail to really *enjoy* something or don't *want* something, you're out of step with the modern zeitgeist, which preaches positivity, entrepreneurship and dynamism. Ultimately, those who lack pleasure and desire may find themselves with a diagnosis of depression. *Anhedonia* – which in Greek literally means 'lack of desire' – is the main diagnostic criterion for depression. In Freud's day, mental disorders were the result of unwittingly wanting something that was forbidden according to the prevailing norms. In fact, he barely mentioned depression. However, in today's command culture, mental disorders are attributed to not wanting *enough* compared to the demands to act, do and experience as much as possible – they are a consequence of our failure to *realize our full potential*. But the upshot is an apparent epidemic of depression among those unable to keep up with the pace and constant demands for self-development.

This is where the religion of the Self can become dangerous because, when external obstacles to our actions are removed, all that remains is our own conscience. If the society around us constantly calls for 'more!' as an ineluctable command, it is easy to become mentally and existentially exhausted. We can always be an *even* better version of ourselves. We are *never* good enough. We always have to do *even* better – to quote the politicians who are seemingly unable just to say 'good' or 'better' without adding that little qualifier. This is where self-optimization takes on a religious aspect.

I think this is where religion, as an existential orientation, can have beneficial effects. It (or Christianity, at least) tells us that we *are* already good enough – no matter how much we give or what we achieve, it is not possible to make ourselves worthy of a heavenly reward. We are doomed to fail, but we are OK anyway. I think this idea is important in our modern command culture – or, at least, it can have highly beneficial effects (if we believe in it, that is). I'm not advocating this because I want a return to old-fashioned, religiously justified bans on all types of behaviour (homosexuality, premarital sex, dancing and alcohol) – God forbid! – but because there is something existentially subversive and psychologically degrading about the command culture's elevation of the Self into a kind of deity (where it becomes the Self with a capital S).

The French sociologist Alain Ehrenberg, who conducted one of the deepest analyses of the multiplicity of depressions of our day, argues that it is precisely this requirement to be ourselves – to perform the Self as a product that can be forever improved – that is behind the depression epidemic.[3] Quite simply, it is existentially exhausting always having to be *the best version of yourself, as often as possible.* Without agencies or authorities other than ourselves, we can only look to the Self. But there is no respite from the Self. I think

that a relevant and altruistic effect of faith may be to provide
that space, simply because it allows us to consider whether
something else might be important – maybe even more
important than us. We might call this many things: God, the
sacred, the demand, the unconditional.

3 April

But what about the effects of faith? What do we know
about them? Let's start with the father of modern positive
psychology, Martin Seligman, and his bestseller *Authentic
Happiness*, an early bible in this field. In it, Seligman lists
five actions, five external circumstances, which we can influence to increase our 'level of happiness'.[4] The first four are:
(1) live in a wealthy democracy, not in an impoverished
dictatorship; (2) get married; (3) avoid negative events and
negative emotion; and (4) acquire a rich social network. By
now, it sounds somewhat optimistic that we should be able
to do all this by using our willpower. But then, he adds the
most important action: (5) Get religion!

It sounds absurd: 'Get religion!' As if it's that simple.
Like a consumer product. Religion as yet another 'thing' we
need to live a happy life. We need a spouse, good friends, a
democratic society – and a religion. This directly articulates
a highly instrumentalized view of religion (not to mention
the other actions on the list), in which religion is positioned
as part of the wellbeing economy and evaluated on the basis
of its positive effect on it. If it turns out that good friends or
a religious outlook on life do *not* make us happier, should
we conclude that they are of no value? That would also
be absurd. And this is where we must be critical of the
instrumentalization of religion: does the value of faith really
depend on the extent to which it brings you happiness or
health? And is it worthless if it doesn't?

Also worthy of consideration is the next list in Seligman's
book, which is about actions that do *not* help you to raise

your 'happiness level'. It is *not* helpful to make more money (above a certain threshold, at least), stay healthy (which will probably surprise many of those for whom health is a religion), take as much education as possible (more education does not in itself generate happiness, but might pave the way for a more sophisticated form of unhappiness), change your race (yes, he did write that!) or move to a sunnier climate. However, Seligman offers some hope by noting various 'internal circumstances' that might make us happier. Most of these consist of practising positive thinking and gratitude, ideas from positive psychology, the main focus of which is on developing techniques for the individual to live well and flourish. I have previously analysed this aspect of positive psychology as a component of the religion of the Self that encourages lifelong self-optimization.[5]

In the context of this book, however, a different question arises: what do we know about the link between happiness and faith? The answer is that it depends entirely on our definitions of the two terms and how we quantify them. One study concludes that one of the scales used to measure happiness (the Oxford Happiness Index) usually identifies a correlation with religiosity, while another (the Depression–Happiness Scale) finds no such correlation.[6] Given the complexity of these phenomena, it is no surprise that it isn't easy to arrive at a clear result. Generally speaking, however, the research is divided into two groups: one that finds no real link between happiness and religion, and one that finds a positive link.

I have not unearthed any studies to suggest that, statistically speaking, religion leads to less happiness – which is good news for the religions of the world. Nonetheless, the results are usually presented only as correlations. This means that the two phenomena go hand in hand, but the direction of causation is unclear. Does believing make us happy, or does happiness make us believe? For example, might it be the case that we are more receptive to the idea of religion when we're happy? We have no way of knowing for sure. And statistically, of course, the results only apply to population groups and not necessarily to each of us as individuals.

Researchers have calculated that more than two-thirds of the Earth's population consider religion important in their everyday lives.[7] Even more – probably about 85 per cent – acknowledge a religious affiliation. If some of the happiness research identifies a significant statistical correlation between happiness and religious beliefs at a global level, then the question is whether it makes sense to extrapolate this conclusion to all of the world's religions and geographic regions. As we delve a little deeper into some of the major studies, it turns out, unsurprisingly, that the picture is more nuanced than that. For example, it seems that religion generally takes up much more space in people's lives when they live in difficult conditions – for example, in countries where food is in short supply and mortality rates are high. In such cases, there is a significantly higher statistical correlation with happiness – or 'subjective wellbeing', as it is often called. In more prosperous countries, not only is religiosity less common but there is less difference between the reported happiness of religious and non-religious people.[8]

It would appear that the benefits of being religious, as measured on happiness scales, depend on where we live. Being religious yields greater dividends in a poor, high-risk society than in a rich, well-functioning democracy. This is in line with the 'comfort-blanket theory' of religion, as mentioned earlier: religion is a source of comfort in the face of tragedy and hardship because it offers meaning and hope. I wonder whether people are becoming more religious in recent days, weeks and months, as the coronavirus runs rampant and we find ourselves physically isolated, with churches not even allowed to hold Easter services? I will probably not be able to answer that question in this book, but we might reasonably conclude that, statistically speaking, the conditions for religion in a rich and reasonably well-functioning society, such as the one I live in (Denmark), will be worse than in poorer and less secure societies. In well-functioning societies, the benefits of faith are probably less obvious because most people are already doing relatively well. In other words, when Danes embrace faith, it isn't to climb the happiness ladder – which in itself would be an absurd argument for religion.

Conversely, we might also say that the present-day religion of the Self often entails a form of sanctification of happiness. In other words, happiness is elevated to a form of salvation, pursued with something resembling religious fervour. In recent years, many observers have noted that we live in an era when we have a duty to be happy.[9] Indeed, a veritable happiness industry stands poised to help the individual to achieve this secularized form of salvation.[10] In traditional Christianity, the purpose of life was to live up to God's expectations of us. In fact, in this life, it was considered impossible to achieve real happiness – *beatitudo perfecta*, as the Christian philosopher Thomas Aquinas called it in the thirteenth century. Rather, it was something that only existed in the afterlife. This idea persisted until the Reformation, which saw an exaltation, almost sanctification, of ordinary life, marriage, family and work. The philosopher Charles Taylor calls this movement 'the affirmation of everyday life' and sees it as fundamental to the whole modern mentality.[11]

During the Renaissance and the Enlightenment, a great shift occurred in the history of ideas, leading to not only the birth of the modern natural sciences but also a shift in the nature of happiness. It was no longer something confined to the heavenly realms, but part of our mortal lives – it even became an intrinsic part of the Self, in which it was associated with good, positive experiences. First, in the nineteenth century, came utilitarianism, the idea of which was to generate as much happiness as possible for as many people as possible. Positive psychology, which emerged at the end of the twentieth century, aims to make people happy in this life rather than in the afterlife. While there is nothing wrong with that per se, it is the consequence of a certain disenchantment with the world, which has relocated the external coordinates of life into the Self, making the individual the sole authority regarding their happiness. If the goal of life is happiness, and if the individual defines what that means, then the individual is effectively a god in their own life – with all of the burdens that entails.

Worshipping happiness in a religious manner as the very meaning of life is closely linked to worshipping the Self – what I have dubbed the religion of the Self. However, it is difficult to relate this idea to what may be considered the core of many religious perspectives: that life is both a *gift* we are given, not something we created ourselves (an idea to which Løgstrup attached great importance in his philosophy), and a *task*, in the sense that there is something we are obliged to do with our lives – an obligation that we do not define for ourselves. I believe that, in many ways, this is what I am seeking in my exploration of religion: an understanding of life as both a gift and a task. And it is difficult to discuss these ideas without invoking some kind of religious language.

17 April

The country has been in lockdown for a long time now because of the pandemic, and I've been exceptionally busy because of it. The University continues to operate – despite numerous obstacles, due to it being physically closed – and I've been on live radio every day discussing the crisis. It hasn't left me much time to think about faith and religion, but I've read various studies about the effects of religion. And since the coronavirus has everybody's attention at the moment, it seems like an appropriate time to look at the relationship between faith and health.

Unless you believe in miracles, prayer isn't going to cure COVID-19. But there's a distinct possibility that religious faith might benefit the immune system. The medical sociologist Aaron Antonovsky proposed his theory of 'the sense of coherence' to shed light on why the ability to find meaning in life and its circumstances can help to ameliorate stressful situations. A world that seems intelligible, manageable and meaningful is one that is good for us psychologically. In fact, such a worldview may even help to counteract stress and depression. It is not unreasonable to think that religion is particularly well suited to providing this sense of meaning.[12]

Researchers have long been interested in whether religious faith has any effect on human health and longevity, and there does appear to be a link. One psychological meta-analysis, which provides an overview of the results from a large number of studies, demonstrated a modest but real negative link between religiosity and symptoms of depression. In other words, significantly fewer symptoms are identified in believers than in non-believers.[13] This is probably relevant to the current situation, in which people are isolated as the virus spreads around the world. It is easy to imagine that having access to another plane – for example, through prayer and the idea of a higher power – might help people to counteract the extremes of depression into which they might otherwise sink.

We don't yet know if there is any link between faith and COVID-19 prognoses. However, a study looking at the link between religious belief and mortality rates for cardiovascular disease concludes that religiosity seems to have a beneficial effect on survival rates.[14] In terms of general health and life expectancy, some researchers have gone as far as to say that 'a religious affiliation is in line with the effects of exercise and avoiding smoking'.[15] While that claim is perhaps ambitiously bold, there is some quite solid evidence that faith has a number of beneficial and quantifiable effects on both physical and mental health. It is difficult to isolate the effects of faith from all sorts of other potential factors – for example, religious people generally smoke and drink less and have a more active social life – and so researchers use statistical tools to account for these other factors.

If the positive effects are not attributable to other lifestyle choices, then either God is protecting the believers (which is hard to believe, let alone verify scientifically), or faith has independent psychological effects on physical health.[16] The latter might be due to what Antonovsky calls 'the sense of coherence'. Those who believe in a divine power and a more meaningful universe may be less prone to the kind of self-reproach that can lead to depression. They may also be more receptive to feelings of joy and gratitude, which in turn reduce stress and anxiety, and certainly have a positive influence on the central nervous and endocrine systems.

While some studies have identified a relatively significant link between religion and health, others show a weaker one – or none at all. Although this is a difficult area to study scientifically, it is probably reasonable to conclude that there seems to be something in religion that makes people healthier. But what about someone who is curious about the concept? Do they have to 'take up religion', just as they might take up running or Pilates, to become healthier and live longer? Again, the instrumental argument starts to sound absurd if it turns faith into a tool for something other than itself (be it happiness, health, longevity, etc.). That makes faith conditional. *If* religion makes me healthier, *then* it has value. Otherwise, it is worthless as an instrument and must be discarded as a defective tool.

Conversely, as we saw in March, there is something appealing in an approach to faith that sees it as something unconditional. If faith is intrinsically about the unconditional, it becomes grotesque to subject it to instrumental conditions. The martyrs who died for their faith would probably find it strange to discuss the value of faith relative to its effect on cholesterol levels. Indeed, their lives were shortened precisely *because* of their unwillingness to renounce their beliefs. Were modern individuals to rely on faith as a means of living longer, it would, in my view, indicate a spiritual impoverishment.

28 April

This month, I have looked at how faith affects various aspects of our lives, such as health and happiness. What remains is, for me, the most central question: is there also a link between religion and personal morality? In extension of the issues I mused on last month, regarding the significance of the unconditional in a religious context, this becomes a crucial question – because morality, too, can be said to be about the unconditional. Back in March, I asserted that it is unconditionally right to use our power over other human beings for their good, at least if we are to take Løgstrup's ethical demand seriously. The demand is not based on 'what's in it for me' but is an unconditional insistence in our interactions with others. Does this mean that there is also a quantifiable, empirical link between morality as something unconditional on the one hand and religion on the other?

Again, the quality of the studies varies, but overall there does seem to be a link. One huge survey of nearly 180,000 respondents from 126 countries concludes that religious people are more likely than others to help a stranger in need.[17] Even in a society where the majority claim to belong to a religion, those who don't consider themselves religious are also more inclined to help strangers. The study, there-fore, concludes that religion seems to play an important role in promoting values that encourage people to help others.

This is good news for the religions of the world – but I find it a little surprising. I must admit that I have long held a prejudice that religious people are generally more judge-mental. That may indeed be the case, but, even so, they are statistically more likely to help in real-world situations.

All sorts of caveats need to be added here, however – does this willingness to help apply mainly to people of the same religion, or is it some form of universal altruism? We don't know. Although I find the research into the links between morality, religion, culture and human actions interesting, intellectual knowledge of the effects of faith is unlikely to make me any more or less religious. Does faith work? Who cares?! That's not the point. It reminds me of studies into parenting and happiness, several of which suggest that having children actually makes us *less* happy – at least while they still live at home. I knew about that research when I became a father, but it would have been ridiculous to use it as the basis for deciding whether to start a family. Who cares?! Having children is a life-changing experience, one that fundamentally alters our existential situation. The idea of making our decision to engage with that experience conditional on its effects on our happiness, health or morality sounds a bit mad.[18]

As mentioned, in the modern era, there is a tendency to instrumentalize everything – even children and faith – and ask, 'What's in it for me?' At the end of this month, I have concluded that there is much to be gained from believing, and that it is definitely worth considering – but that is not why we should do it. If religion is to have a place in my life, it mustn't be just another wellness technique or a tool for self-optimization.

May

Can science replace religion?

1 May

I haven't brought my three children up with religion. Neither has their mum, my wife, even though she still retains the faith with which she grew up. But, based on the broad definition I explored in February – religion as a designation for the symbols and rituals that bind the individual to the community – then our family is very much religious. We baptised the kids, we tied the knot in a church, we celebrate Christmas in the traditional way with hymns, and generally play our part in society's ongoing perpetuation of itself through rituals and special occasions. It is probably more accurate to say that I haven't raised my family with a *particular* religion, even though baptism is sufficient to make them part of the club – at least according to my theologically savvy friends.

I have chosen a different path, trying to instil in my children a fundamental sense of wonder at the world of which we are part – a wonder I have always had. We've taken them to all kinds of museums of art, culture and natural history, at home and abroad. Luckily, they've never grown tired of it or refused to come with us. We've read aloud all kinds of science books for the young, on everything from birth and death to sunshine and rain. We've watched countless documentaries about wildlife, galaxies and solar systems. They know popular science broadcasters and writers like Neil deGrasse Tyson and Bill Bryson better than religious voices such as the four evangelists in the Bible. I've encouraged them to read Bryson's *A Brief History of Almost Everything*, but never suggested that they read anything by religious writers. All three have gone through a phase of wanting to be astronomers. Right now, it is the youngest's turn – our 11-year-old daughter. The celestial bodies have a mysterious hold on children's imaginations. Years ago, our eldest son asked me whether anyone could be an astrophysicist. I replied, honestly, that you need a Ph.D, which is very difficult to get, so it isn't a job just anyone can walk into. Upon hearing that there was a risk that he might not be able to pursue his dream of a research career in astronomy, the 8-year-old burst into tears. These days, he wants to be a writer.

Until now, I've never really thought about whether this interest in science, cosmology and philosophy that I have sought to pass on might have been a kind of substitute for religion. Maybe it has – both in my life and in theirs – and so my question this month is whether, in some circumstances, science acts as a substitute for religion. Perhaps it is even a kind of religion in itself. I could have posed the opposite question – can religion be scientific? – but that would be less interesting. As far as I'm concerned, the moment religion tries to be science, it disqualifies itself and becomes totally uninteresting. For example, 'intelligent design', which is presented as an alternative to evolutionary theory and postulates that life was created by an intelligent force, a god, is pure pseudoscience. The same applies, of course, to literal readings of the Bible that conclude that the Earth is 6–7,000 years old – a far cry from the well-substantiated scientific estimates that lie in the region of 4,500,000,000 years (and the universe is far older than that!). It's an easy enough conclusion to reach that religion shouldn't be presented as science. But it's far more difficult to determine whether the sciences can be a form of religion, so that will be the question I explore this month.

2 May

I am partial to well-written, popular science books about disciplines other than my own. One of my favourites is *A Brief History of Nearly Everything* by Bill Bryson, whom I mentioned earlier.[1] In it, Bryson provides a succinct account of the evolution of the universe, Earth, life and humankind over the approximately 13.8 billion years since the Big Bang. The introduction is a fine example of well-composed science writing, and yet, when I first read it, I also found myself having a rather intense emotional reaction. Allow me to quote a few lines:

> Welcome. And congratulations. I am delighted that you could make it. Getting here wasn't easy, I know. In fact, I suspect it was a little tougher than you realize.
>
> To begin with, for you to be here now, trillions of drifting atoms had somehow to assemble in an intricate and intriguingly obliging manner to create you. It's an arrangement so specialised and particular that it has never been tried before and will only exist this once. For the next many years (we hope), these tiny particles will uncomplainingly engage in all the billions of deft, cooperative efforts necessary to keep you intact and let you experience the supremely agreeable but generally underappreciated state known as existence.
>
> Why atoms take this trouble is a bit of a puzzle. Being you is not a gratifying experience at the atomic level. For all their devoted attention, your atoms don't actually care about you – indeed, they don't even know that you are there. They don't even know that they are there. They are mindless particles, after all, and not even themselves alive. (It is a slightly arresting notion that if you were to pick yourself apart with tweezers, one atom at a time, you would produce a mound of fine atomic dust, none of which had ever been alive but all of which had once been

you.) Yet somehow, for the period of your existence, they will answer to a single overarching impulse: to keep you you.

And so the introduction continues – page after page about all of the coincidences and improbabilities that had to interact to form the Solar System, our planet, life, the species, DNA strands and, not least, the specific and unique combination of events and molecules that have allowed *me* to exist.

On the one hand, the book consists of sober presentations of scientific facts. On the other, Bryson uses words like 'delight' when he draws existential conclusions. There is every reason to rejoice, to be amazed, to be awestruck when it hits you just how big and old the universe is and how small and incidental you are in it. Concepts such as delight and awe are used in hymns and religious writing to describe human relationships with God and Creation. When I first read the introduction to Bryson's book many years ago, I found myself similarly overwhelmed and brimming with gratitude. Just think – we exist! Imagine the countless, complex processes in the universe that had to happen for me to be sitting here reading *these* very words right *now*! It really is unique.

Bryson's book was a global bestseller, and the mass appeal of science in the modern world is not just a consequence of the amazing technologies that humans have devised based on their knowledge of physics and chemistry. I also think it stems from an elementary joy and pleasure in understanding how the world works. Aristotle believed that there were different kinds of knowledge. On the one hand, he outlined two types of practical knowledge: *instrumental*, in which an activity produces something external to itself (for example, a cobbler knows how to make shoes, but the act of making them does not have value in itself), and *ethical*, in which the action is its own justification and has intrinsic value (cf. the Good Samaritan, who did the right thing even though there was nothing in it for him). Aristotle also outlines another kind of theoretical knowledge that, interestingly enough, *also* constitutes its own justification and, as such, is also an end in itself. One of the examples he offers is astronomy because, for beings such as us, knowledge of the celestial bodies is an end in itself. We can derive deep joy from this kind of knowledge, not *despite* its lack of practical application, but *because* of it. Aristotle believed that this was what differentiated humans from animals (or at least from *other* animals). Animals' limited reason means that their minds are restricted to survival mode, whereas the human brain allows us to act and learn for no other purpose than the act of doing so. For humankind, knowledge and actions can be ends in themselves – we are unique in terms of our ability to derive pleasure from seemingly pointless activities.

Evolutionary psychologists have often sought to justify human religiosity by saying that believing in a deeper meaning or a higher power actually increases our chance of survival. And maybe it does. In which case, religious ideas *are* useful, albeit on a deeper level of which we are generally not aware. However, I prefer to take my lead from Aristotle, whose thinking suggests that the value of religion should not be judged on the basis of such Darwinist effects. Instead, we should say that it is incredible that the universe exists and that I exist in it. And it is incredible that humans have been able to generate knowledge about the universe, despite the fact that there is no requirement for this knowledge to help us to be productive, survive or be the best possible version of ourselves.

If religion is about the unconditional, then there is a clear link to the unconditional search for truth that should be the hallmark of science. There is value in research that results in growth, patents and wealth. Of course there is. But pure science has unconditional value simply by virtue of its search for the truth. Knowing the age of the universe or recognizing how minuscule we are in the grand scheme of

things may not make us better off financially, but that kind
of knowledge about our place in the cosmos helps us to grow
spiritually. Is this not precisely the kind of reflection that
religion is supposed to inspire in us so that we may (to quote
William James again) acquire a 'total reaction upon life'? In
that case, there may, in fact, be a surprisingly large overlap
between science and religion. Suddenly, science starts to
look like a kind of religion.

3 May

Earlier in the month, I mentioned two writers and broadcasters who are now arguably more famous than the scientists whose research they convey to the public. Bill Bryson,
as we have just seen, is an exceptionally good writer. Neil
deGrasse Tyson is not only a popular communicator but also
an active researcher in astrophysics and head of the Hayden
Planetarium in New York. I am reading his short popular
science book *Astrophysics for People in a Hurry*, which is
an excellent example of how science communication and
implicit religiosity can flow into one another. And I say this
not as a critique of Tyson but to note that his perspective
can teach us something important about both science and
religion.

Let me cite a couple of passages from the book, which
illustrate what I mean. The very first sentence reads: 'In the
beginning, nearly fourteen billion years ago, all the space
and all the matter and all the energy of the known universe
was contained in a volume less than one-trillionth the size
of the period that ends this sentence.'[2] Just look at the full
stop and try to grasp the concept. It's staggering. And it
must have been a conscious decision on Tyson's part to
use the introduction 'In the beginning', which inevitably
evokes the first sentence of the Bible: 'In the beginning, God
created the heaven and the earth.' Genesis in the Bible is
mysterious – what, exactly, does it mean that 'darkness was

upon the face of the deep', that 'the Spirit of God moved upon the face of the waters', and that 'there was light'? We don't know. This is both poetry and metaphysics. But it's no less mysterious than when Tyson says, in line with current physics theories, that the whole known universe in the beginning – just before the Big Bang, when light came into being – was gathered in a single point so small and so heavy that it is impossible for humans to comprehend. We can read and understand the meaning of the actual words he uses, but it is still a staggering concept.

I do not wish to suggest that the author of the Book of Genesis – be it Moses or someone else – had a particular intuition about the creation of the world that was miraculously similar to the scientific consensus several millennia later. Nor is it fair to call Tyson's description of physics religious, as it is based on observation and measurement, on methodical mathematical and logical reasoning, and, as such, is completely different to a religious text. Nevertheless, both pieces of writing offer a remarkably similar poetic depiction of the incomprehensible nature of the universe. And let's take this line of thinking further: the phenomena we can observe today – trees swaying in the wind, the Moon waxing and waning – can be described by laws of nature that, according to physics, have no permanent validity but are manifestations of gravity, electromagnetic energy and weak and strong nuclear forces. Matter and energy warp space and time, and physicists talk about dark matter and dark energy in ways that make sense in theoretical models but not in terms of our everyday perceptions of reality.

Physics texts are not religious in the ordinary sense, of course, but they sometimes border on the metaphysical. Indeed, it is likely that they affect the reader in a manner similar to religious texts in that they offer glimpses of the universe seen from the perspective of eternity. In 1917, the religious historian Rudolf Otto described 'the holy' as *mysterium tremendum et fascinans* – a mystery that leads to trembling and fascination. This is the special attribute of the holy, which Otto also called the *numinous* – the irrational, profoundly moving aspect of religion, which he compared with its ethical and rational dimensions.[3]

There is something indisputably numinous about physics' version of the creation story, which may well turn our thoughts towards the holy.

Tyson's short book on astrophysics ends with a reflection on what he calls 'the cosmic perspective'. At this point, his writing becomes at least spiritual, if not downright religious. We can say, without stretching the concept too far, that he certainly conveys an understanding of the holy, perhaps without even being fully aware of it. For example, he writes about the cosmic perspective:

> The cosmic perspective is humble.
> The cosmic perspective is spiritual – even redemptive – but not religious.
> The cosmic perspective enables us to grasp, in the same thought, the large and the small. . . .
> The cosmic perspective opens our eyes to the universe, not as a benevolent cradle meant to nurture life, but as a cold, lonely, hazardous place, forcing us to reassess the value of all humans to one another.
> The cosmic perspective shows Earth to be a mote. But it's a precious mote and, for the moment, it's the only home we have. . . .
> The cosmic perspective enables us to see beyond our circumstances, allowing us to transcend the primal search for food, shelter, and a mate.[4]

You can almost hear these words being chanted in unison by a scientifically minded congregation before sallying forth to spread the gospel. There are eleven such commandments in Tyson's book – one more than from Moses. Although Tyson denies that his perspective is religious, it is at least

spiritually and ethically based and probably intended to produce the same numinous emotions as religion – humility, a
feeling of 'redemption, wonder and fascination'.

As a fellow researcher and scientist, I understand that
it is important for Tyson to distance his perspective from
that of religion. However, reading his words, the distance
seems more rhetorical than substantive. There is no doubt
that he sees the cosmic-scientific perspective as beneficial to
humankind. Not just because it generates new knowledge,
but also because this knowledge enables us to show greater
solidarity with each other – and means that we feel we have a
duty to each other. I don't know whether that is actually the
case, but it might be interesting to conduct studies similar
to those I mentioned in April, looking into whether the
scientific, cosmic perspective makes people as loving and
generous as traditional religious convictions.

Tyson's central message is that the universe doesn't
'revolve around us' – literally or figuratively – an insight that
might be said to form the starting point for 'a total reaction
upon life', which in practice can be difficult to distinguish
from a religious one. The overall message is: 'You are an
interesting and important being because you exist. But at
the same time, it is not all about you.' I find it hard to
imagine a more true and edifying thought.

4 May

The famous Danish physicist Holger Bech Nielsen works
with an idea he calls 'God in quotation marks'.[5] The concept proposes a strong and direct link between physics and
theology, and clearly describes how science and religion flow
into each other. I must admit that I don't entirely agree with
everything Nielsen says about theoretical physics, and his
theories have been quite controversial among his peers, but
I do find it interesting when a physicist finds the concept
of God relevant, not only as part of their personal faith (as

many physicists have professed throughout history), but as a necessary part of our scientific understanding of the world.

'God in quotation marks' is Nielsen's term for the agency he believes must exist in the universe, which directs the world towards its own specific objectives. In this context, God is an active force that influences the course of history. Nielsen compares this to the CEO of a big company who tries to minimize a deficit in the accounts. The aim is to ensure the best possible outcome by thinking ahead and projecting future revenue and expenditure.

But what, exactly, is this God seeking to achieve? Bech Nielsen claims that the purpose corresponds to the physics equivalent of 'balancing the books'. It is what he calls the 'minimum contribution to the imaginary part of the action'. This is a difficult idea to grasp but refers to a complex mathematical concept that describes all possible versions of reality, including those that are purely imagined. To arrive at exactly the world that we know, in all its improbability, the imaginary part of the action must be minimized. And God (in quotation marks) will actively seek to prevent anything that threatens this. A few years ago, physicists attempted to find the Higgs boson, which became popularly known as 'the God particle'. Nielsen asserted at the time that, if they were successful, it would trigger an imbalance in the imaginary side of the formula – and 'God' would take action to pre- vent versions of reality that generate large numbers of Higgs particles. He claims that this is evident in the fact that the particle accelerator was struck by a series of problems, which he interprets as 'God's' intervention. Although it has since been possible to identify the Higgs particle, Nielsen believes that there are many instances in which 'God' has influenced historical events so that they move in one particular 'balanc- ing' direction, rather than in others.

Drawing inspiration from Nielsen's cosmic perspective, we can begin to explore the idea of whether humanity itself has a purpose. Perhaps we are here for a reason – possibly to do our bit to minimize the imaginary part of the action. This may sound a little boring compared to traditional religions' grand plans for humanity, but it may turn out to be crucial. Consider this: the universe seems to keep expanding, which it has been doing since the Big Bang, nearly 14 billion years ago. This means that, one day, the stars will all burn out, the temperature everywhere will approach absolute zero, and everything will grind to a halt – a universe in stasis. It will forever be cold, empty and dark – that is, if the concept of 'forever' means anything at all when time itself has effectively stopped. Everything will end.

Physicists call this scenario the *Big Freeze*, and it seems to enjoy widespread support in scientific circles. But the very idea that everything will fizzle out like this and that nothing will ever happen again is enough to give you a headache or anxiety, or both. *Aaaargh!* But this is where Nielsen's theory might offer some hope. He suggests that humankind may have been created by 'God' precisely to create a 'vacuum bomb', which will cause 'the universe to explode and obliterate itself because the bubble will spread throughout the universe. In this way, it will make the universe contract again. I have sometimes dreamt – but this may not be the most credible part of the theory – that humanity may even have been created to make sure that this happens.'[6]

I am not qualified to comment on the physics in Nielsen's theories. From my layperson's perspective, the idea of humankind's purpose in this cosmic game seems absurd, albeit in a fun and thought-provoking way. I mention it merely to emphasize how much religion and parts of science can overlap – in this case, cosmology and physics. I can't, in all honesty, claim to grasp everything that Nielsen is saying, but that's not the point either. Nor is it any different from saying that I don't really get biblical proclamations about the apocalypse and the role of humankind in it. We are probably at the limit of human understanding in general when it comes to both the creation and the destruction of the universe, but that should not, of course, deter us from producing religious narratives, mathematical models and artistic interpretations of these cosmic events. If Aristotle is correct, one of humankind's finest attributes is our capacity to think such apparently futile thoughts.

These ideas become relevant to religious psychology if the attempts by Tyson and Nielsen to share the scientific perspective can be said to generate the same kind of resonance, humility, joy and gratitude regarding our place in the incomprehensibly large universe that religious texts and practices have traditionally sought to convey. Physics is not religion, but can have implications for our relationship with the world that are comparable with religion.

18 May

It's no coincidence that I've spent most of this month thinking about physics. After all, physics is the scientific discipline that basically deals with 'everything' – from the vast cosmic dimensions to the tiniest components of our world. My point is not that science and religion are the same but that there is a surprisingly large overlap – at least in terms of how the two perspectives can inform an individual's approach to questions of existence. Historically, physics has found itself in conflict with religion less often than biology, geology and palaeontology – the sciences that study the Earth and evolution. They diverge markedly from the words of the Bible. A literal interpretation of the scriptures makes Charles Darwin's theory of evolution impossible. And if the Bible holds the truth about Earth's evolution, the geologist Alfred Wegener's analyses, from 1912, of continental drift or plate tectonics can't be credible, either. But they are. So how do we reconcile the modern evolutionary sciences with religion? Is it even possible?

The theory of evolution is one of three major 'blows' delivered by the sciences – at least according to Freud, who saw them as corrections to humankind's inherent narcissism. The first such blow came from astronomy when Copernicus declared in the early sixteenth century that it was not Earth but the Sun that was the centre of the Solar System. The second great blow came with Darwin's theory of evolution in the mid nineteenth century, which demonstrated that the existence of the human being – and all other species – is a result of natural selection processes rather than a creator's master plan. The third blow, claimed Freud – in all modesty – was the one he himself had delivered around 1900 in the form of psychoanalysis, which unseated consciousness and reason from their throne as the guiding principles of human life and replaced them with the unconscious and 'drives'. Together, these three ideas form the pillars of the modern scientific worldview: the Earth is not the centre of the universe, humanity is not the exalted protagonist of historical evolution, and the individual is not even the boss of their own life. However, despite challenging its role, Freud didn't fully reject reason. After all, the three insights (blows) came about precisely by deploying reason.

Darwin's theory was a particular shock for our human self-image in a Christian culture, in which people had become accustomed to the idea that they were created by an almighty God and put on Earth to name the species and rule over the animals. Suddenly, we were animals, too – just another species doing its best to survive in a hostile world in which others care as little about us as we do about deep-sea fish.

In the nineteenth century, the wife of a British bishop (allegedly – although the origins have faded slightly into the mists of history) famously said of Darwin's theory, 'Descended from the apes! My dear, let us hope that it is not true, but if it is, let us pray that it will not become generally known.' Her words reveal a spiritual and moral concern that being 'descended from the apes' would lead to disintegration and nihilism, as we would have no special dignity or obligation as human beings (incidentally, *Homo sapiens* is not descended from the apes, although we share a common ancestor with modern apes). However, I find her response illogical. It is not hard to maintain that human nature – with all that it entails in terms of reason, morality, empathy, etc. – retains just as much dignity whether it is the result of evolution or a one-off act by an almighty God. Would we be more committed to caring for our children, playing our part in the community and loving our neighbour if it was God's will rather than the result of evolution? In principle, I don't think so. On the other hand, although we might fear the wrath of God if we defy His commandments, 'evolution' has no wrath. So, has the idea of our Lord as a great disciplinarian served as a necessary bulwark against indifference to morals and values? As I said in March, I can't accept that idea of God. If the concept of a God is to be justified, it must be a God who insists weakly, and not a strong God who threatens hellfire. The latter, in my eyes, requires superstition rather than faith.

In terms of religious worldviews, perhaps there is a little more convergence between natural history and the Christian faith than the preceding discussion might suggest. After all, Christianity, like the theory of evolution, is about life. In the Bible, man is an 'earthly being' – indeed, the name Adam is supposedly derived from the Hebrew *adamah*, which means arable land.[7] 'For dust thou art, and unto dust shalt thou return' (Genesis 3.19). In this interpretation of Christianity, the human being is not a lonely soul in a physical prison. In an article on Christianity and the theory of evolution, the theologian Niels Henrik Gregersen writes: 'The Earth is where humankind lives, the body is the articulation of that species, and the other living beings are its co-creations.'[8] He believes it is possible to accept evolutionary theory in full and still leave room for religion.

The two perspectives point to different dimensions – science asks *how* the world works, *how* humankind has evolved. Religion asks *why* the world is the way it is and what the *meaning is* of our existence. Science seeks *explanation*, religion seeks *clarification*. This is reminiscent of James' view of religion as humankind's 'total reaction upon the world', which requires existential clarification. Science is tasked with explaining how the universe and humanity have evolved, but clarifying the importance of these conditions for our lives is religion's domain. If we take Gregersen at his word, this suggests, for example, that Tyson's 'cosmic perspective', as discussed above, falls under both science and religion – since, in a way, it combines both explanation and clarification.

I also believe that evolutionary theory can teach us about humility *precisely* because we are not the centre of the universe or history. We belong to a much larger, far older and much deeper world than the one that we encounter on a day-to-day basis. The fact that we can *think* about this and relate to it is what is special about humans. We are not intrinsically special. No species is. But humans have the capacity to acknowledge that fact – which in itself is perhaps an elevated position? This understanding puts us in a position to take responsibility for the planet as a whole, for the climate and for biodiversity. Whales and bees probably don't care whether humans exist, but humans (can) care if whales and bees exist. And not just to exploit them (through extracting resources such as whale oil or honey), but simply because we realize that the world is richer and more beautiful with these creatures in it – whether we use them for our own gain or not. This in itself reflects a kind of religious impulse that various ecological movements have sought to recognize and amplify. We need that impulse and to acknowledge that we as human beings do not exist *in opposition to* nature – we *are* nature. We are the part of nature that knows that it is part of nature, which means we have a special responsibility to care for it.

Gregersen believes that our thinking about this idea should also include reflection on the finiteness of life. We should not make extending biological life our highest objective since we will all die, and death is a prerequisite for making room for other lives. He believes that our current obsession with the boundless extension of life is, in fact, tantamount to a sin.[9] We want more, more, more – not just *in* life, but also *from* life. In this perspective, it is not that death is the consequence of sin (the Fall of Man), but, conversely, that denying the necessity of death is a form of sin. This does not mean that we should celebrate death in a nihilistic way, but it does mean that we should replace an anthropocentric worldview – in which everything revolves around humankind and our goals – with a biocentric one that seeks to perpetuate biological life in all its diversity.

As with physics, there is a significant overlap between science and religion when it comes to the theory of evolution. Both physics and biology position humankind in a larger world that has the potential to fill us with humility, awe and a sense of responsibility towards the whole of which we form a part. Nevertheless, in my eyes, it is important to talk of an 'overlap' and not of science as a religion. Even though religion is not scientific, there is nothing to be gained from attempting to turn science into a religion. It is in the nature of science to be critical and irreverent. For scientists, nothing is sacred, nor should it be. They must be willing to reject everything. But when human beings live their lives, this can't be their only attitude to the world. It can't be our 'total reaction upon life', as we must, of necessity, prize certain things more highly than others, contemplate the meaning of life and seek meaning in what we experience. We need to provide explanation *and* clarification. Science must be allowed to think that my love for my children is nothing more than a result of my selfish genes' attempting to reproduce themselves in organisms we call offspring (although, even in strictly scientific terms, I consider this theory primitive and reductionist). But I can't live my life like that. Pure scientific understanding does not clarify the nature of love or offer guidance on how to cope with parenthood. I need to consider my responsibility for my children as unconditional, and relate to love as more than just electrochemical signals in my central nervous system.

If the unconditional and the holy are synonymous, there must be something holy in our lives. We may be able to formulate scientific explanations for why *Homo sapiens* developed religious ideas, but this is no different from formulating theories as to why we have ideas about evolutionary theory. The theory of evolution can still be justified and correct, even though it takes human consciousness in its very specific form to articulate it. Similarly, ideas regarding the holy and the unconditional may also be valid, even though we arrive at them by virtue of our particular evolutionary and cultural make-up. Our ideas may well be right, even if they are the products of a particular back story.

19 May

Having reread the previous section, I see how challenging it is. In brief, my conclusion to this month's question is that science may well lead to religious reflection on life – indeed, given our knowledge of physics and evolutionary biology, it is almost inevitable that we should seek to clarify humankind's 'total reaction upon the world'. But that's not the same as elevating physics or biology to the status of a religion. In the course of history, it has sometimes been suggested that scientists should replace priests. One such proposal came from the philosopher and sociologist Auguste Comte in the first half of the nineteenth century. Comte came up with new concepts such as sociology (the science of social life), altruism (selfless deeds) and, not least, positivism – which in this context is not about thinking positive thoughts, but about science only dealing with what can be empirically observed and studied.

Like other early sociologists, Comte was interested in the role of religion as an integrating force, but he believed that

traditional religions such as Catholicism should be replaced
by a new, science-based religion: the Religion of Humanity.
The idea was to facilitate human progress on the basis of
altruistic and scientific ideals. Indeed, a number of posi-
tivist denominations and 'ethical churches' were founded
around the world. To this day, the flag of Brazil bears a
motto derived from Comte's Religion of Humanity: *Ordem e
Progresso* (Order and Progress).

Personally, I shudder at the idea of fundamental social
values being conceived of and dictated by scientists or
other experts, no matter how ethical and humanist they
might purport to be. Perhaps it is important that there
is something outside of our ordinary forms of rationality
and scientific methods that offers a wider perspective on
humankind? This is one of the ideas from which religion
derives its justification. It is conceivable that we need something other than ourselves in order to see ourselves. But this
'other' doesn't have to be a metaphysical force or a personal
god – even if, for most people, it probably will be. It could
also just be believing in the 'folly' of helping our neighbour
without expecting anything in return. Perhaps the Religion
of Humanity should have advocated that we count up all
our good deeds in an attempt to ensure the health and
happiness of as many people as possible – like the utilitarian
indexes of wellbeing that some organizations and countries
have started to compile.

June

Does the soul exist?

2 June

I'm on the early-morning Copenhagen train again. For the first time in almost three months, I'm travelling outside of the city where I work (Aalborg in the north of Denmark). It's been decades since I've travelled so little. The country has been in lockdown due to the pandemic but is slowly opening up again. We are allowed to work and move around as before, but not gather in large groups. Having said that, lockdown rules keep changing the ways in which we interact (or don't), both at work and in our leisure time, so maybe the last couple of sentences will be out of date soon. Infection rates may explode again, resulting in new lockdowns, or the virus may vanish, either dying out in the summer heat or being stopped in its tracks by the vaccine now said to be arriving later this year. No one knows for sure.

During lockdown, I've done a lot of radio and social media about the human and social consequences of the virus. It's tempting to let the pandemic dominate this book, too, but I intend to resist that urge and confine myself to brief mentions in passing. We mustn't let COVID monopolize our thinking. People need to ask themselves other important questions – ones that may have been overlooked in recent months. Three different publishers have encouraged me to write a 'pandemic book', but I've turned them all down. I'd rather continue my current research and writing projects – including this book.

This month, I want to look at the soul. Is there such a thing? What is it? I have spent time in the previous months exploring relatively unknown territory (unknown to me, at least), but the question of the soul is much closer to my own discipline of psychology, although we rarely refer to it as such, preferring terms like the mind or psyche. That is what defines psychology as a science – i.e. its object of study is the psyche – albeit the discipline has always found this object notoriously difficult to define. Psychology inherited the problem of the soul from both philosophy and religion but sought to approach it scientifically, using natural science methodology. I suspect that something has been lost in the process. When we talk about a person's *soul*, we are dealing with ideas such as dignity, inviolability, the holy. That kind of thing. But when we're dealing with a person's *psyche*, we are concerned with the mechanics of the mind, information processing and cognition. We are dealing with phenomena and processes that researchers try to recreate and simulate digitally – that is, in machines without souls.

If the soul does exist, then we need a different language to discuss it than one derived from contemporary psychology, neuroscience or computer science. Neither the brain nor a computer has a soul. But maybe people do. My best take is that, to comprehend the soul, we need to use religious language. It is probably no coincidence that virtually all religions thematize the soul in one way or another. Of course, they disagree about its specific characteristics, in terms of immortality, reincarnation, etc., but they do agree that the human being is not an empty machine or some kind of robot made of meat.

Only scientists – including certain psychologists – would talk about humans as highly complex machines. Even if, intellectually, they *think* this is the case, I very much doubt that they *live* their lives on the basis of that position. The idea may be possible scientifically, but not ethically or existentially. The soul is essential for life. But what *is* it? Does the soul even exist? This is a central question in my year with God. And the answer to the question may also be one of the best justifications for the importance of the religious dimension: that we need it to understand what is significant about *us*, about *people* – that is, the spiritual or psychological aspect of our being.

3 June

Back in January, I quoted one of my favourite philosophers, Ludwig Wittgenstein, who said he wasn't religious but couldn't help but approach every problem from a religious point of view. The same applies to the question of whether human beings have souls. Wittgenstein offered an enlightening remark on the topic, which sparked this month's reflections. In his posthumously published *Philosophical Investigations* (1953), he writes: 'My attitude towards him is an attitude to a soul. I am not of the *opinion* that he has a soul.'[1]

When we meet other people, the question 'Does he or she have a soul?' is, in a sense, too direct. We rarely ask it. The exception is the metaphorical use of the word. For example, we might ask if a musician has soul, in which case we are talking about how much feeling they put into their playing. As to whether my fellow human beings have a soul, I don't have a theory about this or a strong intellectual conviction. The same applies to the question of my own soul. But I relate to others and to myself as if we do. I think Wittgenstein identifies something profound in the quote above: the question of the soul doesn't belong to discussions about what exists in the world (cars, tables, chairs, flowers, bicycles – and souls?), but to the ethical and existential dimensions of life, which are about how we live and behave.

Is the soul perhaps a specifically human, binding way of behaving, rather than an inner 'object' we carry around with us? Should we approach the soul as we do God (as discussed in March)? In other words, we should not expect to find 'something' that *exists*: an object that we can call God or the soul. But we can discover that something *insists*, calls to us, demands something of us, in a way that appears to originate outside of us. I think that's what we mean when we talk about the human soul. The soul isn't made up of the body, the organism, the brain, the psyche or mind, as elements in the natural world. Instead, the word implies that the human being is an entity fundamentally different from an inanimate object or a machine. Humans are not objects or machines, precisely because they have a soul. A machine is a system in which the individual elements can be separated and reassembled without impeding the machine's functions. But we can't take apart a living being without killing it. That which disappears we might call the soul, and machines don't have one.

When Wittgenstein said that our attitude towards another person is an attitude to a soul, I think he meant that we don't just observe each other as objects, like the balls on a pool table. We're not just detached *spectators* watching each other's lives. We don't simply rely on our knowledge of neuroscience or psychology to predict and control other people's behaviour. We're not just interested in the causal factors that drive people to act in a certain way. We're also *participants* in each other's lives.[2] As such, our main interest is why they think or do something – and there is a difference between a cause and a reason. Causes are what drive us, often without us even realizing it. It could be childhood trauma, a surge of adrenaline or an undetected brain tumour. Reasons, on the other hand, are what we refer to when we *justify* our actions. We help our fellow human beings because there is good reason to do so. As far as we know, humans are the only living beings capable of justifying their own actions.

We are capable of more than just posing objectifying questions like the psychoanalytical 'What unconscious forces drove you to do that?' This is a question asked purely from the perspective of a spectator and assumes the other person is a machine, powered by fuel (e.g. mental energy) and made of mechanical parts (e.g. urges and the superego). We can, instead, relate to them as fellow participants. In fact, this is the basis of our relationship with the other – we care what they want from us, what their actions mean and whether there is a reason for them. It is a matter of relating to them on a *spiritual* rather than *mechanical* level. This is absolutely fundamental to concepts such as morality, law and democracy. If people have no reasons for their actions, or if the reasons are unknowable to others, it doesn't make sense to punish them or allow them to participate in democracy.

It is a legitimate fear that the increasing use of the spectator perspective, based on scientific insights, will reduce humans to machines bound by a system of cause and effect, thereby eliminating responsibility and guilt. If our behaviour is attributable to causal factors, there's nothing we can do about it. It is a prerequisite for actions, responsibilities and reasons that we relate to the other as a soul. Unless we perceive the other as a being that chooses to act, as a participant in our shared life, there are no *actions*, only *behaviour*. This probably isn't the aspect of the soul that interests most people, though. I would hazard a guess that they probably care more about the question of immortality, so I will return to that.

8 June

Our perception of the soul is made up of myriad ideas from religion, science and pop psychology. And they are often mutually contradictory. We don't have a single concept of the soul – not even if 'we' only means the West. Rather, we have a whole host of concepts and ideas that intersect with and influence each other, and which are embroiled in an ongoing struggle for dominance. I once wrote a short text about the soul – its philosophy and psychology – for a book in Danish that translates as *50 Ideas that Changed the World*.[3] I will present a reworked summary of it here, hopefully offering a brief overview of the soul's place in the history of ideas and opening up a discussion about its importance to faith and religion.

Western concepts of the soul have their roots partly in ancient Greece, partly in Christianity. The Greek word for the soul was *psūchê*. In Greek mythology, Psūchê was a goddess married to the god of love, Eros. She is usually depicted with butterfly wings, which are often interpreted as symbolizing the elusive, fragile nature of the soul. Should you try to grab hold of this creature with your clumsy fingers, it will lose its power and ability to fly. This image of the fine and delicate soul contrasts with the coarse physical body. Psūchê and Eros also had a daughter, Hedone, the goddess of pleasure and delight.

For the Greek philosophers, Psūchê did not represent the soul in the Christian sense, nor the mind as the seat of thoughts and emotions. In *On the Soul*, Aristotle analyses the soul as a biological concept, as the first principle of life. He believed that all living things – animals, plants, people – have souls simply by virtue of being alive. It is the plant's soul that allows it to turn its leaves towards the sun. However, the word *psūchê* also means breath – death literally follows your last breath. Aristotle believed that the soul is the form of the living body, which also means it cannot exist without the body. The soul is made up of the abilities and dispositions that collectively characterize the living body. The soul allows us to think, speak, feel and act. For Aristotle, it would make as little sense for the soul to exist without the body as it would for the ability to walk to exist without feet and legs. The human soul is also distinguished from that of plants and animals by dint of rationality – i.e. we can relate to our thoughts and actions and, for example, seek to improve them if there is good reason to do so. The fact that we have a rational soul means that we can be held accountable for our actions. This corresponds well with my emphasis on the participant perspective.

Aristotle's teacher, Plato, had depicted the soul somewhat differently, as our immortal essence. For Plato, a human being consists of a body and a soul, but the soul essentially *is* the human being. When the body dies, the soul lives on. This is why Socrates, the protagonist of most of Plato's dialogues, is able to face death without fear after being convicted of impiety and corrupting the young. Socrates believed in the eternal nature of the soul, which provides comfort during our finite, mortal lives here on Earth, where the body is the prison of the soul.

For Plato, then, the soul is something you *are*, whereas, for Aristotle, it is something you *have*. According to Plato, I am my soul, and I have a kind of intimate and private sense of it inside me. Aristotle, on the other hand, asserts that 'soul' describes what I can do while alive – it is the sum total of my abilities and functions. Plato, therefore, inspired the many philosophers and scientists who have since envisaged the soul as a form of inner consciousness with which one is assumed to be identified as an individual (and which, for some religious people, exists for all eternity). Conversely, Aristotle has inspired those who believe that the soul consists of the rational abilities and dispositions of living people, but with which they are not identical. The disagreement regarding the nature of the soul between these two giants of ancient Greek philosophy remains unresolved more than two millennia later.

Christianity's concept of the soul is more complex than is often thought. The simplistic idea of an eternal, intangible substance in a material body is actually quite difficult to find in biblical texts. Nor is it readily apparent in the work of the most important Christian philosophers – for example, Augustine in the fourth century (who largely follows in Plato's footsteps) and Aquinas in the thirteenth (who follows in Aristotle's). Nonetheless, the idea persists, like something learned as a child – especially in the United States – of the immortal soul that lives on when the body dies.

In fact, Christian theology places great emphasis on the resurrection of the flesh, the implication of which is that eternal life is not purely spiritual in nature. When we are resurrected after death, our bodies will also rise again. Christian thought is, therefore, more integrative (the soul and body belong together) than dualistic (the soul and body exist independently of each other). In other words, it appears to have more in common with Aristotle than with Plato.

The concept of dualism is closely associated with the seventeenth-century philosopher René Descartes. But even his early thoughts about dualism are open to interpretation, and more nuanced than they may seem at first glance. He saw the soul as synonymous with consciousness, and divided the world into two fundamentally different substances: spatially extended *matter*, on the one hand; and *mind* (consciousness or the soul), on the other. In effect, Descartes situated the outer world in the human soul, and thought that the only things humans ever truly perceive are the ideas lodged in the consciousness. He saw the mind as a kind of container for certain experiences (called ideas), which are presumed to correspond to phenomena in the outer world. However, we can only ever *assume* this – we can never *know* – because if the only thing we can know is the content of the soul, then everything else (the outer world, the existence of other people) becomes purely hypothetical, and we have no reason whatsoever to believe that anything else exists other than the content of our own consciousness, our own soul. This absurd conclusion is called *solipsism*: that my own soul (my own subjective experience) is all that exists. It is all too easy to arrive at this conclusion if we identify the soul with our inner consciousness.

Descartes had to perform mental gymnastics to try to avoid the inevitable solipsistic conclusion to which his own starting point led. Among other things, he had to argue that God existed because, for him, God was a necessary guarantor that our experience corresponds to something in the outer world. Descartes also had to embark on a – to put it mildly – difficult quest for the precise location where the soul and the body interact. He thought he had found it in the pineal gland (a small, pine-cone-shaped structure in the human brain that we now know regulates the sleep hormone melatonin). This quest reduced him to an almost comic figure, a scapegoat for virtually every problem in Western philosophy. But, on closer inspection, his theory of the soul is more sophisticated than its reputation might suggest. At one point, for example, Descartes writes that the soul belongs to the body as a whole and can't be attributed to individual parts of it – a far cry from the simplistic pineal gland theory.

Why did philosophers such as Descartes start to identify the soul with consciousness and claim that it could accommodate the whole world? The answer is probably that, at that time, the nascent natural sciences were engaged in a larger project of demystifying the world. The world that both Plato and Aristotle saw as full of purpose, meaning and value was increasingly seen as a mechanical system governed by blind laws of nature. As the world was demystified, the soul-as-consciousness had to be mystified to accommodate all that is significant in life (meaning, values, etc.). This became the basic assumption for much of the philosophy to follow. Since the world no longer had a soul and had become mechanical, human consciousness needed a soul.

Ever since, one of the fundamental questions in Western culture has been how to find room for the soul in a scientific view of the world. Many have argued that it's impossible and, therefore, there is no such thing as a soul. One proponent of this view was the philosopher Julien Offray de la Mettrie, who, as early as the eighteenth century, made a provocative case for pure materialism with the book *L'homme machine* (Man a Machine). Numerous philosophers and scientists also drew inspiration from Darwin's theory of evolution, and the same ideas echo throughout modern neuroscience. For proponents of total materialism, spiritual phenomena are simply processes in the brain and central nervous system. According to the most radical materialists, any talk of the soul is based on a flawed theory (it simply doesn't exist), and we should purge our language of references to the soul and consciousness. Goodbye participant perspective, hello human machine.

Others, however – including myself – insist that we need the idea of the soul, no matter what science says about the brain. As a hypothesis about what may or may not exist ('there is a soul'), the idea is, of course, open to debate. However, as a practical principle, it is possibly essential. That is what Wittgenstein means when he says, 'My attitude towards him is an attitude to a soul. I am not of the *opinion* that he has a soul.' The fact that the other is a being with a soul, who is capable of taking action and worthy of esteem and recognition, reflects a fundamental and innate attitude that plays an essential role in the mutual intertwining of our lives. It is a kind of 'spontaneous manifestation of life', as Løgstrup called it. In *theory*, we can reduce humans – both others and ourselves – to nothing but biological machines, nerve processes or complex configurations of molecules. But, in *practice*, we can't. Existentially, it is impossible to approach others like that, except perhaps in extraordinary circumstances, e.g. in relation to people suffering from severe dementia. But, even in such extreme cases, we (thankfully) can't completely eliminate our inclination to approach the other as a soul.

Wittgenstein continues: 'The human body is the best picture of the human soul.' We see the soul of the other in the face, facial expressions, gestures and mannerisms. This brings us back to Aristotle, for whom the soul is not an inner, private substance hidden behind the bodily exterior. Rather, it is the very ability of the living person to think, feel and act. We have a form of practical knowledge about all of this. It is only when we turn the soul into a hidden substance, lacking physical form, that we allow ourselves to look for it somewhere inside us, in the consciousness or via brain scans. It is, of course, impossible to find. The soul does not exist as an object inside us. It can't be seen with an MRI machine. If Aristotle and Wittgenstein are correct, you will not find the soul anywhere, simply because it doesn't exist in a 'place'. As a concept that describes our abilities and dispositions, the soul can no more be traced to a single location (for example, the brain) than a house's ability to be a home can be traced solely to its doors, roof or furnishings. The soul is a characteristic of the human as a whole, much like being a home is a characteristic of the house as a whole.

16 June

I hope readers have stuck with me through this long discussion of the history of ideas about the soul. I know that it has been heavy going, and also that it leaves the biggest questions about the soul unanswered: Is the soul eternal and immortal? Can it be reincarnated?

As always, when it comes to matters of faith and religion, the individual will, of course, gravitate towards the answers that they consider the most correct and edifying. Many will want to believe in the immortality of the soul – either to reduce the fear of their own death or to seek solace when others shuffle off this mortal coil. If the soul is eternal, then, in a sense, our loved ones are not truly dead, and we live in the hope that we might meet them again. It is not for anyone – and certainly not me – to shatter somebody else's faith. But I will try to explain why, following much deliberation, I have concluded that this idea of the soul isn't credible. And even if it were, it would diminish that which has fundamental value in human life, including love and freedom.

First, the idea of the eternal soul lacks credibility because we have no idea how this ethereal substance could possibly survive the death of the organism and exist independently of the body. The idea of an immortal soul is at odds with everything science tells us about the world. I think Aristotle was on to something: the soul can't exist without the living body because it is simply a word to describe the abilities of the body. No physical body equals no soul. But this doesn't mean that the soul can be reduced to the body. This is no more mystical than pointing out that the value of a banknote can't be reduced to paper and ink.

The idea of the immortal soul also lacks credibility because it assumes that I *am* my soul and, therefore, that I am immortal if my soul is. But if you think about it, that's a pretty strange idea. How could *who I am* – the sum total of all my relationships, my entire history, my links to my community and society more broadly, this physical body and everything else that collectively constitutes the being known as Svend Brinkmann – be identical to some kind of ethereal substance? When I die, the thread of my life will be cut, my physical body will decompose. You will no longer be able to talk to me or detect my presence, simply because I will no longer be here. Even if it were possible to imagine that there is some kind of soul atom or substance that lives on after the death of my body, I would have no reason to believe that this substance was *me*. Because who I am is a creature living *this* life. I am the life I live. Since this life has an end, it is of no concern to me whether something abstract about me continues afterwards – because whatever that is, it is not *me*.

I have similar issues with the idea of reincarnation or the transmigration of souls. Even if there was a soul that could be reborn in a new body or another person, why should that hold any meaning whatsoever for me? What would that soul have to do with me? It wouldn't have my relationships, my duties, my dreams or my mortgage. There are people who claim to have lived past lives, usually as exceptional individuals such as kings and queens. But it makes no sense to say that *I* was a king, because *I* am Svend Brinkmann, who was born in 1975 in Denmark and has lived the life I have lived.

And even if my soul had existed in Napoleon's body prior to taking up residence in mine, what possible significance could that have for me? None at all.

Similarly, I find the idea of my soul being reborn after my death completely uninteresting. After all, it wouldn't be me being reborn but some depersonalized substance. We might as well say that my body's atoms will return to the natural cycle after my death and find their way into other living organisms – which is a real possibility. The point is that this idea is just as impersonal – and in a certain sense, matters just as little – as the idea of the rebirth of some kind of eternal soul. All in all, therefore, I agree with Aristotle: the body and the soul are inextricably linked. On the other hand, there is something meaningful about the hope of physical resurrection because it would be the whole person who returns – flesh, blood, bones and all. It's just hard to believe.

In a certain sense, I find the idea of physical resurrection and eternal life harmful. Why harmful? Well, if resurrection and eternal life were a reality, it would diminish all that we consider significant in life. Given enough time, everything that has meaning and value will disappear. Various thinkers throughout history have put forward this idea, one of the most recent being the philosopher and literary scholar Martin Hägglund.[4] His book *This Life*, a widely acclaimed study of what he calls *secular faith* and spiritual freedom, argues that, for something to have value, it must be ephemeral. This applies to objects, projects and people. It applies to ourselves and to other people. It is about life itself. We commit to our lives and take care of what has meaning and significance. And things only have meaning and significance precisely because they do *not* last forever.

According to Hägglund, the dream of eternal life would actually be a nightmare. It would be a state in which nothing could have meaning, nothing could motivate us, nothing could spark our interest. If we lived forever, there would never be any reason to do one thing rather than another because everything could be done and undone an infinite number of times, and nothing would be lost. Hägglund, like others before him (perhaps most explicitly, the German philosopher Martin Heidegger), notes that our lives are temporal and finite. And, if I am the life I live, then I too am temporal and finite. Finiteness structures everything I do and everything that happens in my life. I don't want to die and disappear, but, at the same time, I don't want my life to last forever. This is the contradiction at the heart of the secular faith that Hägglund investigates: the belief that we must and shall dedicate ourselves to a life that will end, which in each and every way is fragile and precisely for that very reason can have infinite value. Something can only have meaning or value because there are differences, and in eternal life all differences are dissolved because there is no temporality.

Hägglund distinguishes between religious faith, which for him is linked to the hope of the eternal, and secular faith, which springs from caring about the fragile lives that we as mortals live with others. He argues that even individuals who are firm believers in the religious sense *must* have a basic secular faith when, for example, they mourn the loss of a loved one. Because if they truly believed in eternity and the overarching value of eternal life, there would be no reason to grieve. In principle, we should be glad that the deceased has moved on to a better place – and some people do indeed claim that this is the case. Nevertheless, the vast majority mourn their loss, which shows that, even as religious individuals, they have a secular belief in the temporal.

Hägglund elegantly flips the objection often directed at atheism: that it, too, presupposes a belief – namely, that there is *no* God. He says to believers that they do ultimately presuppose unavoidable finiteness by committing to and being bound to a life along with other people. According to Hägglund, the reality of loss and fragility is a prerequisite for our lives and obligations. If the religious individual really loves someone, if they truly care about something or are committed to a cause, then that is only possible because they hold a secular belief that life is finite. Finiteness is a prerequisite for everything that is worthy of love and commitment. If there were an almighty God who could preserve everything for all time and remove all risk of suffering and death for all eternity, then there would be no meaning and no value.

I agree with much of what Hägglund has to say but perhaps stop short of his conceptual distinction between secular and religious faith. This may work if you believe that religion is necessarily about the afterlife and the immortal soul. However, as I discovered earlier in the year, in my exploration of the theology of the 'weak' God, religion can also be said to stem from the basic conditions of existence – that we and others will definitely die, and that from this fragile mortality emerges an unconditional demand to engage in life and help others. Hägglund would (rightly) say that this perspective is fundamental to meaning and value, but can nevertheless be classed as religious. It implies a belief in something that cannot be scientifically proven (that there is something we are called to do, even though we are not rewarded for our efforts), and which is organized and conveyed by churches or church-like communities, some of which have been perpetuating this narrative for generations.

17 June

I don't think there's much more to be said about the soul. On the one hand, it is a religious concept, long since abandoned by philosophy, psychology and science in general. On the other hand, it is a concept with a kind of existential necessity and doesn't need to be linked to grandiose notions of infinity and eternal life. In fact, I have argued that there is good reason to see the soul as being inextricably linked to the body – and therefore to mortality and the inevitable fragility of life. It is precisely the fact that we will die that endows life with its meaning and makes other people irreplaceable. So when we talk about the soul, I don't think we are talking about something supernatural or metaphysical. But we are talking about humans as more than mere machines or biological organisms. Following Wittgenstein's lead, we ought to approach each other as souls because humans, as spiritual beings, invoke a different kind of esteem and respect than do objects and machines, for example.

I recently read a Facebook post by the 83-year-old theologian, and student of Løgstrup, Ole Jensen, which I have been given permission to cite:

> Regarding the debate about atheism, we must not forget the many who call themselves 'religiously tone deaf' or the likes – often ruefully. They want to 'be able' to 'believe' and remain members of the church. It sounds like the word 'deference', which means that something stops them: here and no further; if they carry on, they'll transgress 'something', and they don't want to do that. To offend is to commit a violation. And that can be 'inexcusable'. Such as draining the will to live from another human being. Taking their self-respect. Taking away a child's will to live. Its joy. This makes the offender 'dishonourable'. And more besides, e.g. preventing people from experiencing pleasure and recharging their batteries in nature. If these words mean something to the 'religiously tone deaf', and that will be the case for most people, we could argue that they are actually religious – let's call it anonymously religious. What the individual concerned lacks is a concept of what religion and faith mean. For example, the misconception that it is about great waves of emotional experience, 'being able to' pray, feeling the presence of God, etc. Christian media are full of testimonies about such emotional experiences. And people are welcome to

them. But they're not prerequisites for being religious. If they were, then I, too, would be 'religiously tone deaf'. Arguing with committed atheists is a waste of energy. Direct more attention to those who call themselves 'religiously tone deaf'! That's my advice to all you apologists. (Ole Jensen, Facebook, 9 June 2020)

Jensen distances himself here from the idea of religion as emotional experiences or practices (e.g. prayer), referring instead to deference – that is, an attitude towards life and to others that can be expressed through concepts such as forgiveness and inviolability. From a scientific worldview, these words make little sense, because forgiveness is just a form of Darwinian dynamic. Ultimately, nothing is inviolable, as everything is just atoms and molecules in motion. But we can't live like that. We have a need for a language that allows us to comprehend the attitude to life that leads us to believe in deference, forgiveness, inviolability. That language is religious, and the soul is central to our ability to understand it. These ideas hold truths, but they cannot be articulated in a scientific language of cause and effect. They are truths that require us to meet them halfway. It is like trust in society – if you constantly question its existence, you are bound to destroy it.[5] As Ernest Hemingway said, 'The best way to find out if you can trust somebody is to trust them' – and the only way we can determine whether humans have a soul is to relate to them as if they do.

My answer to this month's question – Is there such a thing as the soul? – is, therefore, yes. It exists, but we will never find it. And it only exists because we never stop looking for it.

July

What can we learn from the Bible?

2 July

I spent June trying to find the soul. I didn't find it – at least I didn't locate any kind of eternal and immortal substance – but I did find it meaningful to say, like Wittgenstein, that our attitude to the other is an attitude to a soul. The point is not that we must find the soul, but that we must keep looking. And this is a task that seems best suited to religious language. But isn't it a bit limiting to look only for the soul? What about the spirit?

Søren Kierkegaard famously distinguished between the soul and the spirit. The soul is psychological, while the spirit is, well, spiritual. But what does that mean? It comes up in the famous introduction to *The Sickness unto Death* (1849), written under the pseudonym Anti-Climacus, but published under the name S. Kierkegaard:

> Man is spirit. But what is spirit? Spirit is the self. But what is the self? The self is a relation which relates itself to its own self, or it is that in the relation [which accounts for it] that the relation relates itself to its own self; the self is not the relation but [consists in the fact] that the relation relates itself to its own self.[1]

The quote may sound rather cryptic,[2] but it's not as impenetrable as it might first appear. First, Kierkegaard defines humankind as spirit rather than soul because many other beings can have a soul (dogs, cats and budgies). But what is the spirit? Kierkegaard asserts that the spirit is the self, which raises a new problem – defining the self. He determines that the self is a relation that relates to itself. In other words, the self is not an object or substance but a relation. But a relation between what? While the answer is not covered in the short quote above, Kierkegaard would say that humankind is both a physical and a mental being – a synthesis of body and soul. Nowadays, we would probably use the terms 'physiological' and 'cognitive'. However, the mere fact that there is a relation between body and soul does not constitute a self in the Kierkegaardian sense. This relation only becomes spiritual, and thus a self, in the act of relating to itself. In other words, the self is neither our psyche nor our physical body, nor the sum of those parts, but the act of relating to the synthesis (or relation) between them.

The spirit is our ability not only to have a relationship with our mind, our body, or the world in general, but to relate to how we relate to them. Because we can relate to how we relate, we are not bound to relate to an issue in any particular way. In this sense, spirit is also freedom. For example, somebody who is prejudiced against Jehovah's Witnesses can also try to relate critically to those prejudices. They can relate to how they relate. This is something humans are capable of as spiritual beings. In Kierkegaard's eyes, this means that being a spiritual being is also angst-inducing because it awakens in us the prospect of freedom. When we relate to how we relate, we understand that we are empowered to make our own choices and that so much could be different. In the Kierkegaardian universe, angst, freedom and spirit are related.

All of the above might be easier for the modern, secular reader to understand were we to substitute the concept of spirit with that of culture.[3] I acknowledge that this would not be in line with Kierkegaard, but it allows us to understand the earlier quote as meaning that human beings, as observed by themselves, are cultural beings. In a broad sense, culture is a designation for conveying a relationship between nature (including the body) and the psychological or spiritual. In this sense, culture is spirit.

The concept of culture comes from the Latin root *cultura*, which means tilling or cultivating. Sometimes, culture is posited as the opposite of nature, but it is probably more accurate to say that culture is a *form of nature* – i.e. a cultivated form. Consider agriculture. Humans have *cultivated* plants and fields for millennia. This is still nature but in a processed form. In this sense, cultural products – art, language, social conventions – are never unnatural. They are just ways in which nature has been cultivated or processed as a means of mediating our relation to it. Culture is, therefore, a mediated relation to the world. In this sense, culture is spiritual because it is about being able to relate to how you relate. Correspondingly, to have a self is to have a mediated relationship to yourself and the world. All animals eat, sleep and reproduce, but only human cultures allow individuals to relate to *how* these activities are performed. As a result, they take different forms in different parts of the world due to different traditions regarding food, family structures and the rhythm of daily life.

If culture represents the great collective spirit, then the individual human self represents a smaller, more discrete spirit, which only exists because the greater spirituality – the culture – has cultivated it. Or, at least, that would be a modern interpretation. According to Kierkegaard, the self does not determine itself – rather, God determines the self as a self-relating relationship. Our spiritually incomparable aspect – our capacity to relate to how we relate – is only possible because God has determined this relationship.

Kierkegaard would no doubt have little time for my secular interpretation that it is the community or culture – at any rate, *other people* – that cultivates our self and our spirit. However, as per modern developmental psychology, I think it is reasonable to say that we do not become reflective selves in an isolated process of self-development but because we relate to ourselves through other people. In order for the tiny, helpless, biological blobs that are newborn humans to become self-relating selves – and, in that sense, become spiritual beings – they must see themselves through the eyes of others. We only learn to relate to ourselves because others have first related to us. In this sense, we owe ourselves, literally, to others. I find it difficult to agree with Kierkegaard that a celestial God is necessary to describe how the spirit is constituted. However, if spirit and culture are truly interchangeable, then we can begin to understand the emphasis in the sociology of religion on the interwoven nature of religion and society. This kind of perspective dates back at least to Durkheim, who believed that religion is simply the name for that which sustains social life.

3 July

What role does the Bible play in relation to discussions about spirituality?

First, if it is true that the Bible has coloured virtually every aspect of human culture, then it has undoubtedly also informed our understanding of the origins of humanity – even for secular developmental psychologists. The Bible, especially the New Testament, is simply part of the language we use when we (at least those of us in the West) try to make sense of the world and ourselves.[4] It is a spiritual text par excellence. The Norwegian author Karl Ove Knausgård, an atheist of sorts, says that for him, the Bible is a way 'to think about what it means to be human. It is one of the great ways of thinking. It is a wonderful tradition.'[5] And he's right. To shed light on what we can learn from the Bible, I will spend this month studying three parts of Christianity's holy book that have been crucial to our perception of psychology, ethics and religion. As morality determines what we consider to be spiritual or uniquely human, it might also be said that these three parts concern the *origin*, *exercise* and *limits* of morality. Precisely what I mean by that will hopefully be made clear in the coming days. Rest assured, I have a plan!

Second, it is worth noting that the Bible has been hugely important to the study of culture. Yesterday, I tried to argue that spirit and culture are virtually synonymous. Indeed, the German philosophical tradition approaches the humanities – the study of literature, art, history, culture, etc. – as a spiritual science, i.e. an area of study ultimately rooted in the desire to understand the Bible. At the end of the eighteenth century, the German theologian Friedrich Schleiermacher pioneered hermeneutics, a method of interpretation explicitly aimed at instilling a well-founded understanding of the holy scriptures. The Bible is probably the most important spiritual resource in Western culture. Kierkegaard's view of soul, body and spirit, as discussed above, would be unthinkable without it. Our concepts of ethics, politics and life, in general, are steeped in biblical ideas. Whether we are believers or not, it is a fact that the Bible has influenced almost every aspect of our worldview. It is relevant, therefore, during my year with God, to turn my attention to the Bible and ask questions: What can we learn from the Bible? Does the Bible have anything to say to me?

First, a little about the text itself. *The Bible* is the collective term for the holy scriptures of both Judaism and Christianity. The Christian Bible is divided into two main parts. The Old Testament is virtually identical to the Hebrew Bible or *Tanakh*. The New Testament consists of the specifically Christian scriptures, including the four Gospels that tell the story of Jesus. These are believed to have been written in 65–95 CE, i.e. at least thirty years after his crucifixion and death.[6] None of the authors was a first-hand witness to the events depicted, but they all drew on oral and written sources. The Gospel of Mark was written first, followed by Matthew and Luke, who used Mark as their template. These three are called the synoptic gospels. The Gospel of John, the fourth and most recent, is somewhat different, as it is not based on the other three. The Old Testament, for its part, consists of a large number of older texts written over a period of approximately 1,000 years, the oldest parts of which date back to 1200 BCE.

Let me begin at the beginning, with the Book of Genesis and the Creation – when God creates Heaven, Earth and humankind. 'And the earth was without form and void, and darkness was upon the face of the deep. And the Spirit of God moved upon the face of the waters.'

And then there was light. Light and life enter the world through God's spirit. Many philosophers since the Greeks have identified a close connection between breath and the spirit – and this is also the case in the Bible. God then created humankind out of clay – from earth we have come, literally – and breathed the 'breath of life' into the nostrils of man so that we came alive. The first man, Adam, was placed in the Garden of Eden, where he could eat from every tree, except for one that provides knowledge of good and evil. Then God created a woman from the man's ribs. They were naked but unashamed. They could not yet be ashamed because they did not know good and evil and could not see themselves from the outside. However, a cunning serpent enticed the woman into eating from the tree of knowledge. All of a sudden, the two humans saw themselves clearly and discovered that they were naked. God punished the serpent, which was cursed to crawl on its belly; the woman would later give birth to her children in pain, and Adam would physically labour 'in the sweat of thy face' until he eventually died and returned to the earth. This was the price of knowing good and evil. Animals don't possess this knowledge, but humans do because we are spiritual beings.

The biblical myth of the expulsion from the Garden of Eden has been a source of inspiration for theoretical analyses of morality, emotions and the Self at the very least since Kierkegaard's *The Concept of Anxiety*.[7] According to

Kierkegaard's famous interpretation, the myth is about existential anxiety in the face of nothingness. It is this anxiety that takes humanity from animal innocence to reflexive consciousness – and, therefore, potentially, awareness of guilt and shame. Unlike fear, which is based on the possibility of a tangible threat, anxiety in an existential sense is directed at the possibility of freedom. According to Kierkegaard, as creatures comprising body, soul and spirit, we are able to conceptualize nothingness as the possibility of the yet-to-be-realized, which is both a precondition for freedom and the basis for anxiety.

The experience of nothingness and anxiety is crystallized in the example of the forbidden fruit. How could Eve and Adam understand why they shouldn't eat the fruit when they had not yet acquired an understanding of good and evil? If we don't know what evil is, we can't know what it means that something is forbidden. In effect, God set a trap for Adam and Eve. Without an understanding of good and evil, the very idea of defying God's will makes no sense and therefore leads to anxiety. At the same time, however, the idea kindles the possibility of freedom. The formula for anxiety is as follows: I must not do this, but I do not know what it means that I must not do it. I, therefore, face the unknown – a nothingness. Only by doing what is forbidden will I know what it means for something to be forbidden. And doing this is my choice – the freedom to choose as a spiritual being manifests itself through anxiety.

The sociologist Jack Katz sees the Creation as not only a cosmological myth, but also a highly concentrated form of social psychology.[8] It shows how the human self was born in guilt and shame and offers a socio-psychological analysis of the challenges we face in our relationships with others.[9] We learn from the myth that the self is born as a reflexive relationship when we see ourselves through the eyes of others, which is a shameful event. It is shameful because the first glimmer of self-reflection (and thus the emergence of the

Self per se) occurs when Adam and Eve realize that they have done something wrong by violating God's command. They then see that they are naked and must cover their bodies with the garments provided by God.

Symbolically, Adam and Eve reach up to the branches of the tree, lured by the serpent, to eat from the tree of knowledge. As a result, they come to understand the concepts of good and evil, right and wrong, and, therefore, guilt and shame. When we ask how Adam and Eve could have been guilty when they had no understanding of good and evil prior to eating the apple, the answer would appear to be that they could not have been. They are only guilty in retrospect, once they shamefully acknowledge the wrongness of their action. The forbidden fruit, Katz concludes, is the process of self-conscious reflection itself.[10] As such, *shame* becomes the fundamental emotion that gives rise to the Self or spirit, and which guides the individual's relationship to the community and other moral emotions. It is through eating the fruit that Adam and Eve become like God, as violating His commandment is their first free and creative act. They become actors who not only are created by a creator, but who, from that moment on, can create and tell their own story. According to the myth, this is the point at which we left behind our state of nature, our naïve innocence – it is the beginning of human history. The spirit is born through fear and shame, and we transition from natural history to cultural history. Adam and Eve must be expelled from the perfection of Eden because, in acquiring divine knowledge of good and evil, they lose their innocence and more closely resemble their creator. From then on, humans are obliged to have an awareness of and act upon this knowledge, on Earth, in mortal bodies – half divine, half animal.

The myth seems to possess some validity as an analogy of the emergence of the human self. It expresses the idea that the self is born in shame and revealed in the eyes of others.

Shame is a bit like looking through a keyhole only to find
that you are being observed by others. The self is exposed
and painfully objectified, and we are unable to control the
presentation of ourselves in the community, which functions as a powerful tool of social control. Paradoxically, it
is through this painful revelation that the self emerges as a
reflexive being. Through shame, the community is no longer
merely an abstraction, but a tangible reality consisting of
basic norms, the breaking of which we instinctively feel is
harmful. If this is correct, it indicates that the biblical story
of the Creation is still remarkably topical – indeed, almost
universally relevant. I think that we can rightly regard the
understanding of freedom and the human self, as expressed
in the Book of Genesis, as the foundation of human psychology, ethics, law and even cultural life per se. Not bad for a
story that's thousands of years old.

4 July

That was the *psychology* of the Bible – about the birth of the
Self or the spirit – but what about *ethics*? First, let me briefly
summarize the earlier discussion of ethics in this book: the
story of the Good Samaritan is arguably the most significant
expression of the radical, compassionate ethics preached by
Jesus. For me, despite its simplicity, it is an inexhaustible
source of reflection.

To recap: in the Gospel of Luke, Jesus tells the story of the
Samaritan to a lawyer who challenges Jesus by asking, 'what
shall I do to inherit eternal life?' The answer is to love God
and everyone else, but the lawyer thinks that is unrealistic.
This is where Jesus tells the story of the Good Samaritan,
who met a man lying half-dead on the road from Jerusalem
to Jericho. The man had been attacked by robbers, and
both a priest and a Levite (a form of assistant in the temple)
passed him by as he lay stricken on the ground. However, a
man from Samaria – one of the traditional enemies of the

Jews – felt sorry for the injured man, cleaned his wounds, bandaged him, and took him to an inn, where he paid the host 2 denari from his own pocket for the man's shelter. The lawyer admits that the Samaritan was a compassionate fellow human who acted in accordance with God's law. 'Go and do thou likewise', Jesus concludes.[11]

The story illustrates the unconditional demand we face when we meet a person in need and have the power to help. This is the most fundamental principle of ethics. But there is also a deeper layer to this story because it is not just the Samaritan who emerges as an example to follow. Upon being told that the path to eternal life is, among other things, to love 'thy neighbour as thyself', the lawyer asks Jesus 'And who is my neighbour?'[12] In other words, he asks Jesus to identify the people to whom he should show compassion. After telling the story, Jesus eventually returns to the question of who the neighbour is. The lawyer himself answers, correctly, 'He that shewed mercy on him' (i.e. the Samaritan). In that reading, therefore, it is not only those in need whom we must love and help. Our fellow human, our neighbour, is also the Samaritan, he who helps![13] And, since the Samaritan represents the enemy, this reveals the radical nature of Christian ethics: we must love our enemy. We must understand that those we despise are also capable of good – but, even if that were not the case, they nonetheless embody an implicit demand to be loved.

It is easy to understand that the poor victim must be loved and helped. But it seems harder to understand that he who may have hurt us and is our enemy must also be loved and helped – even if we don't get anything in return. The imperative to help is *categorical*, as Kant later said in the eighteenth century. It is not a transactional matter: 'If I do such and such, then I achieve this or that.' Rather, it is 'I must love and help the other.' Full stop. Jesus repeatedly emphasizes this, probably most famously in the Sermon on the Mount from the Gospel of Matthew:

> But I say unto you, Love your enemies, bless them that curse you . . . That ye may be the children of your Father which is in heaven: for he maketh his sun to rise on the evil and on the good, and sendeth rain on the just and on the unjust. For if ye love them which love you, what reward have ye? . . . Be ye therefore perfect, even as your Father which is in heaven is perfect.[14]

The message is, then, do the right thing, without reservation, without conditions. Therein lies the Kingdom of God.

Earlier this year, I placed great emphasis on this basic ethical understanding. I consider it a religious concept in that it breaks with everything that can be justified empirically or scientifically, and yet there is something inescapable about it. The problem, however, is that it is so radical that it seems impossible. I don't know anyone who loves everybody, let alone their enemies. Most of us, at some time or another, lapse into vengeance and pettiness. So what's the point of attempting to adhere to an ethical system to which we can never measure up?

It is on this point that various theologians have critiqued my take on human ethics in my previous books (e.g. *Stand Firm*, *Standpoints* and *The Joy of Missing Out*). Their argument is that if, as I do, we place the ethical demand on human shoulders alone, the burden becomes heavier than is good for us. Faced with the radical demand to love our enemies, we may find ourselves totally paralysed by our own inadequacies. Many of us will recognize this sensation, since the feeling of inadequacy is probably the modern human's most common affliction. In April, I analysed the new form of morality in which social norms are not primarily based on prohibitions ('thou shalt not!'), but commands ('you must do both this and that!') to which we are constantly subjected. This phenomenon is also termed the 'competitive' or 'performance' society, and it is very likely that there is a causal link between this particular aspect of the zeitgeist and the high prevalence of stress, anxiety and depression in young people.

This is where the religious perspective is particularly relevant. I would like to see the ethical (in a broad sense) as that which provides standpoints, or anchors, from which the modern human being can reject all sorts of problematic commands and demands. However, the difficulty arises when the ethical becomes an impossible task for which we humans are inadequately equipped. Does this mean that ethics risk becoming an arena in which we must be competitive in an attempt to be as good as possible – or even better? Companies already use corporate social responsibility as a competitive parameter, and there are suggestions that something similar occurs between individuals when they compete to have the 'right' attitudes, adopt the most ecological and sustainable way of life, and generally indulge in virtue signalling. However, it is often overlooked that, in modern society, being good can be quite (financially) expensive. As a result, the rich find it easier to be good and thus feel in a position to shame the poor for their fecklessness.

This is where the Bible not only offers an ethic that renders us inadequate (and it does!), but also tells us that we are forgiven for being so. As human beings, we can't fail to act wrongly and hurt others – and yet, at a much deeper level, we are good enough as we are. As I said earlier, we can't make ourselves worthy of the Kingdom of God by being good because the moment we do good for our own benefit, we have made goodness conditional. It is then no longer unconditionally good, and therefore not a reflection of the Kingdom of God. Quite the ethical paradox.

An important aspect of the Bible's message (more precisely, Jesus' message) is that we may be inadequate, but we can be forgiven for it. According to Jesus, this is because God is merciful. But if God is not an otherworldly being sitting on a cloud, passing judgement, like an American president issuing pardons on a whim, and rather is a symbol of the

unconditionality of life, can we still make sense of mercy
and forgiveness? Perhaps, if we understand that forgiveness
itself is equally unconditional and that, as human beings,
we must try to live by it – not because we are taking part in
a forgiveness competition, but because to forgive has value
per se.

The philosopher Jacques Derrida offered a famous – and
quite challenging – analysis of the phenomenon of forgiveness. He simply states: 'forgiveness only forgives the unforgivable'.[15] His reasoning is quite simple: if something is
forgivable, there is no reason to forgive it. Only that which
is unforgivable requires forgiveness. Forgiveness is, therefore, only possible by virtue of its impossibility. Conversely,
forgiveness is impossible, which is precisely what makes
it possible.[16] This is not just a silly play on words but a
deep insight into a fundamental human phenomenon. It
succinctly expresses what is meant by the philosophical
term *aporia*. The concept, which stems from the Greek word
for puzzlement, signifies a form of deadlock or stalemate.
Only by action – not by even more analysis – can deadlock
be broken. In other words, we must forgive. According to
Derrida, forgiveness (if genuine) has no purpose; it is unconditional and aimless (in the literal sense of having no aim
in mind). It cuts through all calculations of what has utility
value and purpose because, if forgiveness is made a means to
something other than itself, it is no longer forgiveness.

Forgiveness is, therefore, a form of benign ethical madness. This can make the idea quite provocative because it
challenges our usual perceptions of fairness, our ideas of
reasonable and understandable behaviour. When the satiri-
cal magazine *Charlie Hebdo* published its first edition after
the terror attack on it in 2015, the front page proclaimed
'Tout est pardonné' (All is forgiven). It was a radical, almost
startling response. It might also be called an ethical one.
Although it may at first appear weak because it doesn't seek
revenge, it actually reflects incredible strength. It echoes

the Sermon on the Mount, in which Jesus says that we must forgive other people their misdeeds. The message is not 'an eye for an eye', but 'Love your enemies, bless them that curse you.'[17]

As far as ethics are concerned, Jesus offers an interpretation that confronts humankind with an ideal that we can never live up to. We are necessarily, intrinsically inadequate. And, for this reason, this kind of ethics necessitates forgiveness. Perhaps this is Christianity's genuinely original contribution to ethics? The existential question then becomes one of how to live in a state of permanent inadequacy without it becoming an excuse. 'I let you down, but, hey, as a human being, I'm fundamentally inadequate, so it doesn't matter, does it? You'll just have to forgive me!' That position represents a warping of ethics. Just as we are not responsible for everything that happens, we are not blameless simply because we are inadequate. Nor are we entitled to *demand* forgiveness from someone else. Sometimes we will genuinely fail, and, when that happens, we can hope – but not demand – that the other forgives us, just as we can hope that we ourselves will forgive the other. Derrida writes that 'forgiveness forgives', emphasizing that it is difficult to *want* to forgive. We don't necessarily make a conscious decision to do so. Sometimes, forgiveness emerges and then becomes pressing – almost like a kind of divine intervention. It is a matter of being open to forgiveness rather than dwelling on thoughts of revenge. We forgive not for some kind of reward, but because to do so has unconditional value.

6 July

My readings of Genesis and what Jesus says (the story of the Good Samaritan and the Sermon on the Mount) tell us something about both who we *are* (beings who can relate to ourselves) and what we *ought to be* (beings who try to live up to the unconditional demand, even as we reflect on our own inadequacy). The Bible is, therefore, a source of both psychology and ethics. As I see it, both can be expressed without a metaphysical belief in an omnipotent, celestial God or the rewards of an imagined afterlife, both of which are otherwise often considered central tenets of religion. The interpretation of the Christian faith I am trying to express says – almost conversely – that it is precisely when we relinquish these traditional tenets that the Bible has something to teach us. If we stick to them, we make faith conditional on omnipotence and eternity. But in my eyes, the teachings of the Bible pave the way for perhaps the most real and meaningful form of faith, because it is only with the death of God – the revelation of the impotence of the Almighty's omnipotence, as symbolized by the Crucifixion – that humankind is called upon to have faith. After that, it's up to us. The Bible's promises of resurrection and eternal life then become about passing down the narrative of the unconditional to succeeding generations.

An acquaintance of mine, a woman in her nineties, whom I have been interviewing regularly for several years, puts it like this: 'From earth you have come, to earth you shall return, and by *words* you shall rise again.'[18] The life of the individual necessarily ends with our biological death, but our words can live on. Today, we can read (versions of) the words of Jesus that were supposedly uttered millennia ago and which have had tremendous significance for billions of people ever since. As Hannah Arendt wrote in *The Life of the Mind*, when asked about the nature of eternal life, Jesus didn't actually mention resurrection. Instead, he said that, if we follow his example, we will find that the Kingdom of God is already in our midst.[19]

But all this doesn't really add up. As I mentioned earlier this year, psychology and ethics are at odds with the religious suspension of ethics. We see this in the Old Testament story of Abraham and Isaac, to which I feel obliged to return one last time. It is an all too familiar tale in which poor old Abraham is put to the toughest test imaginable when God tells him to go to Moriah and sacrifice his only son, Isaac, on a pyre. The scene unfolds with cold, almost eerie detachment.

Isaac says to his father, 'Behold the fire and the wood: but where is the lamb for a burnt offering?'

Abraham replies, 'My son, God will provide himself a lamb for a burnt offering.'[20]

(Remember, he's talking to *his own child*, whom he's about to put to death.)

As Abraham raises his hand, holding a butcher's knife, over his son's prone body, he hears a voice from heaven, an angel, proclaiming that he must not hurt the boy after all. The angel explains God's intention in terms that may appear to be madness: 'because thou hast done this thing, and hast not withheld thy son, thine only son: That in blessing I will bless thee, and in multiplying I will multiply thy seed as the stars of the heaven, and as the sand which is upon the sea shore.'[21]

This is the God of the Old Testament talking. It is the strong, omnipotent God who makes a conditional deal with Abraham. Precisely *because* Abraham was willing to sacrifice everything for God, the Creator will shower him with riches. It is the ultimate statement of strong theology: God as a kind of mafia boss who puts His subjects to the test and rewards their unflinching obedience. This is the kind of theology that provides a breeding ground for fundamentalism, which requires us to sacrifice our ethics – or even other people – in the name of God. I know wise men and women of the cloth who will argue that Abraham lifts the knife secure in the knowledge that Isaac will be spared and that this means God is above human ethical concerns. I think that detracts from the story. If Abraham is certain that his son will not be harmed, then it is not truly a sacrifice, and the story doesn't really matter.

I have already mentioned how Kierkegaard, in *Fear and Trembling*, looks upon Abraham positively precisely because he obeys God and rejects the ethical demand. In Kierkegaard's eyes, ethics may be disregarded in the service of a higher purpose. I have argued that the only thing that can be above ethics is something else ethical, because 'good', to use Murdoch's terms, is a sovereign concept that we can never transcend or disregard. Something ethically *good* can only be trumped by something ethically *better*. If, according to the Bible, Abraham is right to agree to sacrifice his son, and thus his ethics, then this too is an ethical choice, albeit one based on higher-order ethics. However, I just don't think it can be considered right because Abraham, through his intended action, reduces Isaac to an object – a means to a higher goal (obeying God). Most of us today would say this is unequivocally wrong. That's not how we would have thought of it in the Old Testament days. But I believe that we, as modern human beings, are on to something, not least because we have also read what Jesus thought about our unconditional duty to our fellow human beings. Through Jesus, Christianity offers the opportunity to see past the father figure – the strong, old-fashioned God. Indeed, at the core of Jesus' teachings is the idea that we should do good not to ingratiate ourselves with the Almighty, but because it has unconditional value per se.

7 July

I revisited the story of Abraham to make the point that life doesn't always make sense. We encounter a variety of conflicting demands and don't always know what is right. The unconditional, the ethical, is not like a mathematical equation for which there is always a correct answer as long as we know all the angles. Ethics are often closer to a maze, where our efforts to find our way out often mean we end up more lost than ever.

The Old Testament story of Abraham was probably not intended to be interpreted the way Kierkegaard does, as a conflict between ethics and the religious. Such a distinction is, in itself, modern. For Abraham, the religious and the ethical were one and the same. It is probably more accurate to say that the conflict is about two kinds of loyalties, or two different duties – to God and to the family. Read in this way, I can make some kind of sense of the seeming madness of Abraham's story by pointing out that life frequently throws up similar dilemmas. However, regarding the question of whether it can be justified to abandon ethics deliberately, my answer will ultimately be the opposite of Kierkegaard's. No. Nothing negates an ethical demand except another ethical demand. In practice, of course, we can (and often do) act in ways that disregard ethics. But when the discussion is focused on the normative – how we *should* act and live – we can't ignore ethics. Even an argument that there are no objective values, and therefore we can just do what we want, is based on normative ideas that it is a good thing to be freed from the oppressive norms that dictate our lives. The argument that it is *better* to be a knight of the faith like Abraham than a boring ethicist must in itself be an ethical argument if it is to have any validity. In the famous words of Levinas, ethics is *first philosophy*. There is no getting around it. In that sense, it is also the starting point for faith, understood as fidelity to the infinite demands of ethics.[22] But I'm repeating myself now. Going round in circles. Perhaps because I'm trying to make sense of this as I write.

To recap: this month, I've tried to describe what I think we can learn from the Bible. It can provide a basic understanding of what kind of being we are as humans (psychological) and to what this being is ultimately committed (ethics). We may find ourselves unsettled by the feeling that life is not a jigsaw puzzle in which all of the pieces fit nicely together, but a confusing mishmash of insoluble dilemmas in response to which we are doomed to make mistakes. To use a term that has fallen out of fashion, we are all, inevitably, sinners.

I have learned all of this, directly or indirectly, from the Good Book. I understand, of course, that many other readers will extract many other theses from the Bible: about God the Almighty, about the resurrection, about eternal life. I see such interpretations as superstition, and they don't harmonize with my view of life. But, unless I've totally misunderstood the Bible's message, none of this is particularly important. The Bible can be read in many ways, and I don't want to attack anyone's faith – nor superstition, for that matter. But the question then becomes: why is it the Bible, of all books, that is so crucial to conveying the message of the unconditional? Why couldn't it be *Harry Potter* or *Star Wars*, both of which are also about good and evil?[23] An essential part of the answer is probably that it is simply due to the Bible's reception history. It is the Bible, and especially the New Testament, that conveyed this message first – and most clearly. Other texts simply follow its lead.

Next month's question may prove a little trickier. If we acknowledge – as I have argued – that we shouldn't interpret God as an almighty superpower, then why would there only be one god, rather than many? If the important thing is that religion and faith make sense and have resonance in our lives, what difference does it make whether we are monotheists or pantheists? Might there perchance even be advantages in believing in multiple 'gods'? It may seem like a strange question to ask in the wake of our discussion of the Bible, but this is the point I have reached.

August

Could there be multiple gods?

24 August

Not only is it August, but it's almost the end of the month –
and seven weeks since I added anything to this book. I had
hoped to get around to it during the summer holidays, but
when they finally came around, I didn't have the slightest
shadow of a doubt in my mind that it would be better to
step away from the keyboard, recharge my batteries and
just be there for the family. We had planned to drive all
over Southern Europe, and I had booked four consecutive
weeks of holiday for the first time ever. But the pandemic
put paid to all that. We spent most of the time in our
holiday home in Denmark. It was nice, even though the
weather was cool and wet most of the time. But at least we
managed to paint the cottage on the dry days. Then, on
the last week of the holiday, with travel restrictions eased,
I had a sudden urge to drive to Amsterdam. I had been
there about twenty-five years ago while interrailing with my
wife. I remembered it as a lovely city with an abundance of
excellent museums and wanted our children to see some of
them. We managed a total of six in five days. An excellent
end to the holidays.

I mention all this because I'd like to start the month by
talking about the first museum we visited. And for good
reason. The Anne Frank House is one of Amsterdam's best-
known landmarks, and I hope that talking about our visit
will help to shed some light on this month's question: could
there be multiple gods? I realize that sounds strange, but
allow me to explain.

As someone from a Christian culture, I have taken monotheism for granted so far. I may have been trying to explore
how someone – *me* – can find meaning in religious faith as
a human being in a modern world informed by science, but
the journey has been based on the unspoken premise that
religious faith means belief in one – and only one – god.
However, in the long history of mankind, this is actually a
relatively new idea. The oldest religious concept is thought
to be *animism* – the belief that nature is endowed with
spirit. It is an idea shared by all of the religions rooted in
hunter-gatherer societies, and seems to precede other and
later concepts such as the afterlife or ancestor worship.[1]

Animism isn't necessarily the same as polytheism – the
existence of multiple gods – because it also allows for a
belief in a single spiritual presence that imbues all nature.
However, the belief that, for example, plants, animals and
natural phenomena such as thunder or rain possess some
form of intentionality (i.e. they have agency and influence)
can quickly start to resemble polytheism and manifest
in different gods who embody, e.g., thunder (Thor), war
(Týr) or fertility (Freyja). Of course, it's not just pagan or
archaic religions like those worshipped by the Vikings or
ancient Greeks that operate with several gods. Hinduism is a
major world religion, with more than 1.25 billion adherents
(although it is also extremely diverse – so much so that not
all Hindus can be called polytheists). I am interested in
what – if anything – we might learn from this polytheistic
perspective.

What exactly, you may be wondering, does any of this have
to do with the Anne Frank House? Well, during our visit, I
had a very intense experience – one so powerful that I think
it may be comparable to the religious experiences adherents
have in their places of worship or ascetics have in the wilder-
ness. Most people know the story of Anne Frank: the young
Jewish girl who first fled Nazi Germany to Amsterdam with
her family, and then hid in an attic for more than two years.

She lived in hiding with her family and a group of other Jewish people until they were discovered by the Gestapo. Anne was then deported and died, purportedly of typhus and starvation, aged just 15, in Bergen-Belsen, only a matter of weeks before British troops liberated the camp. While in hiding in Amsterdam, she kept a diary and wrote various other pieces, which were published after the war at the behest of her father, Otto Frank – the only member of her family to survive the Holocaust. *The Diary of a Young Girl* went on to be one of the most widely read books in the world.

The museum does audio tours. You start on the lower floors, listening to the story of both the Frank family and the other victims, and make your way up until you finally reach the small attic rooms where they hid.

It is deeply moving, especially seeing the many photographs and even a film clip of Anne as a young girl, full of life. In a truly profound way, you almost feel that she is still present in the house. Anne Frank was a gifted, forthright and expressive child, and clearly a talented writer for her age. For me, however, the most moving part of the hour-long tour was a recording by Otto Frank – the old man who had lost his wife and children – speaking of his love for his daughter. He explained that he hadn't read the diary while Anne was alive because he had promised not to. He calmly yet sorrowfully recalls how, after the war, he was surprised to read Anne's notes and how it struck him that parents never truly know their own children. For some reason, this touched me very deeply. I wasn't really myself for the next few hours, as we walked around Amsterdam and talked about the visit with our own children.

The atmosphere in Anne Frank's house is, of course, very sombre, almost subdued. You are shocked that people can bring themselves to kill innocent men, women and children simply because of their religion and ethnicity. At the same time, the place also has a distinct air of defiance. I can't find a better word for it than that. Visiting her house is a kind of defiance because Anne's *joie de vivre* remains irrepressible and contagious, despite her mental and physical torment at the hands of the Nazis. Today, it isn't Nazi edifices that radiate human strength and value, but this humble place where a young girl hid as she wrote her diary.

I know it's a word to be used with care, but there's something almost divine about Anne Frank, or the memory of her that lives on, and about the house where she lived and wrote until she was taken prisoner. Visitors encounter an atmosphere, a gravitas and an existential depth that can only be expressed in religious language. I wonder if that's what animists and polytheists mean when they talk about places and objects being imbued with spirit? Is this a phenomenon that I – a secularized child of the Enlightenment – can also experience in a house in Amsterdam? Apparently so. Can I conceptualize it in scientific language and a rational framework? That is something I would like to find out.

25 August

In February, I introduced the sociologist Hartmut Rosa's illuminating concept of resonance: the state of being in harmony, or in a conversation, with the world. Resonance is when we experience the world as not just consisting of inanimate elements devoid of meaning, but as something that responds to us. If the world can 'respond', surely there must be a something or someone listening and answering? I know that sounds strange, but maybe the world *is* strange. As mentioned earlier, Rosa understands religion as the idea that there is something that is 'responsive, accommodating and understanding'. Not a 'something' that just reflects or echoes me, the individual – that would be the same as me just listening to myself – but a presence that helps me to experience meaning and generates resonance.

Although the atmosphere in Anne Frank's house is the result of unimaginable tragedy, the resonance is undeniable.

It demands the visitor's attention, immerses us in history and confronts us with the depths of human immorality. And yet, at the same time, it is edifying. It testifies that a young girl can be so strong and defiant that she still speaks to us across decades and generations. Perhaps this is what animistic or polytheistic religions seek to convey when they talk about gods or spirits in streams, animals or temples? I don't believe in that sort of thing – at least, not literally – but I do believe that the world allows itself to be experienced as responsive. And I believe in the importance of atmospheres – like the one in Anne's house – that make it possible for us to fathom the unfathomable, at least for a fleeting moment.

Re-reading the last few sentences, I worry that I may be getting carried away! I've no desire to turn into one of those New Age types of whom I am so sceptical. Luckily, numerous philosophers have written about these phenomena in a sober and analytical way. I am thinking in particular of the book *All Things Shining: Reading the Western Classics to Find Meaning in a Secular Age* by Hubert Dreyfus and Sean Kelly.[2] Dreyfus died in 2017 after a long and distinguished career teaching philosophy – in particular Heidegger – to American students. He is particularly well known for his critique of artificial intelligence. Dreyfus believed that only a living being that exists in the world with a body and with genuine interests in what is going on can be said to possess intelligence and consciousness. Co-author Sean Kelly was one of Dreyfus' students and is today an eminent professor of philosophy at Harvard, with a background in mathematics, computer science and linguistics. Neither is exactly a fuzzy thinker or prone to wishy-washy spiritual fads. Yet their book argues for a kind of polytheism. The fact that two enlightened, highly rational philosophers believe in the existence of multiple gods is quite astounding – what, exactly, are they suggesting?

They are primarily concerned about the nihilism that they see as endemic in the modern world, especially in the West.

Today, many people believe that the world is fundamentally meaningless and that any meaning in our lives is the result of our own free choices. There *is* no meaning, so we must *create* it ourselves. As the book's title suggests, the two authors believe that our world is no longer full of 'shining things'. We have lost our concepts of the holy and the sacrosanct. However, they also point out, right at the outset, that we can still experience something 'luminous', even if only in glimpses, e.g. in a heroic deed. They describe an incident on the New York subway when one man rescued another who had fallen on to the tracks just before a train arrived. People who perform such deeds almost always say that they had no choice. The implication is that these acts of heroism don't spring *from* the actors involved, but almost flow *through* them, a bit like some kind of divine intervention. Anyone who witnesses such an incident will understand that they are dealing with something deeply meaningful and admirable. This assessment is not something we *choose* to believe, but a direct reflection of our experience in the moment (just as we don't choose to perceive a Mozart aria as melodic – it just is – or a rose as red). Dreyfus and Kelly think we place too much emphasis on *choice* in modern culture, and pay too little attention to existential situations in which something external in the world acts through us or reveals itself to us in a certain way – be it on the New York subway or in the Anne Frank House.

So far, so good. But what does all of that have to do with polytheism? Dreyfus and Kelly go all the way back to Homer and the Greeks' understanding of the many gods. Perhaps God is dead, as Nietzsche wrote in the late 1800s – at least in the philosophical sense of an overarching, absolute cosmic focal point – but perhaps the lesser gods are still with us. Dreyfus and Kelly are particularly interested in the characters in *The Iliad* and *The Odyssey*, whom Homer described not as being driven by inner, private experiences and convictions, but as engaged in external, collective moods or atmospheres. The Homeric heroes lived in a world charged with meaning and importance. For them, life was about being attuned to these meanings and being moved by them. This echoes Rosa's concept of religious experience as a form of resonance – as a harmonious relationship with that which may be considered holy.[3]

In Dreyfus and Kelly's eyes, people have a need for gods because they help us to understand that we are at our best when we act in ways we have not quite chosen, or that are out of our control. This doesn't mean that we are (or ought to be) irresponsible. It means we should strive to be subjects of that which is good. We don't create the good ourselves, but – as they somewhat poetically put it – we can let it 'flow through us'. They use 'gods' as shorthand for everything that is outside us – that which transcends us and demands our wonder or gratitude. Gratitude, in particular, is a feeling that is inaccessible, at least in principle, to nihilists who believe that the individual is the source of all values. To be genuinely grateful requires that something other than ourselves is responsible for the existence of that which is good, true or beautiful.

On numerous occasions, Homer emphasized the profound significance of sleep as an example of something that can't be achieved simply by trying harder. Sleep occurs whenever it wants, although it can be kind to us – in which case, we must show gratitude to Hypnos, the god of sleep. Even if we want to fall asleep, we can't usually *choose* to do so. However, this doesn't mean we're utterly powerless, because we can, of course, prepare ourselves for it as well as possible. Phenomena such as sleep, the sudden compulsion to forgive, the love we feel for another, the tears that fall when we witness a kind gesture or hear a beautiful piece of music – all of these are the gods stirring something within us. To be moved by the Anne Frank House is to hear the gods speak to us.

The gods always come from the outside and help us to find harmony in certain situations. And some individuals

embody this special quality and illuminate something in
the world. Dreyfus and Kelly mention Marilyn Monroe and
Roger Federer. I would add Anne Frank. They may not be
particularly powerful metaphysical beings, but they capture
the attention of an entire culture and create moving moods
or atmospheres in their own unique ways. According to
Dreyfus and Kelly, a god (in the Homerian sense) is a feeling
or mood that directs us towards what is most important in
the world and allows us to respond in the right way without
thinking about it.[4] The gods who do this are countless and
exist everywhere that people come together to engage with
important matters. Perhaps this interpretation of the gods
is digestible even for scientifically minded types like myself.

26 August

I'm not going to start believing in the gods of Hinduism or
the Norse Aesir. Not even the gods of Olympus, despite my
deep affection for Greek antiquity. But I do think it is appropriate to talk about the elementary and familiar phenomena
in our lives – instances when we are moved or influenced
by atmospheres and situations – in polytheistic terms. Just
as I find little value in a literal reading of the Bible, I find
polytheism almost meaningless when taken at face value.
Conversely, just as I believe that the Bible is a fundamental
and meaningful work for understanding human existence,
at least in our part of the world, I also believe that there
is something important and meaningful in the polytheistic
idea that the world consists of myriad forces and movements
that are worth listening to and allowing yourself to be influenced by. The modern, individualistic idea from psychology
– that we only have access to the world via our own inner
experiences (our 'mental representations') and that each of
us is capable of controlling what meaning and value this
life has – I find nihilistic. It is the idea that makes us all
miniature, omnipotent gods in our own right. It permeates

much of pop psychology and the self-help industry, which makes money from promoting ideas like: 'You can do what you want' and 'Happiness is a choice.' These motivational slogans elevate the individual to an almighty force capable of deciding about its life and determining its own success. This perspective is absolutely alien to polytheism, in which our lives play out in situations – from great historical dramas to small, everyday events – that we did not create but can try to understand.

Dreyfus and Kelly argue, convincingly, that the gods serve as a concept that allows us to understand the core of the human phenomenon and how we can be moved by moods and situations. On the other hand, they also discuss the monotheistic notion of a single, unifying deity. I would like to address this briefly because I am rather sceptical about the idea that all religions and mythologies can be mixed and matched. How do we account for the previously discussed idea of (the weak) God while also taking polytheism seriously?

Dreyfus and Kelly's answer is that Greek polytheism contains the seeds of the monotheism that has been so important for the cultural development of our part of the world over the last couple of thousand years. They describe Zeus – the head Greek god – as the source of all meaningful cultural practices. While there are individual gods of war, love, farming, etc., all of these activities are in a way held together by a force that the Greeks called Zeus. The same idea, they argue, underpins the Judaeo-Christian idea of God as the father. They interpret Herman Melville's fantastic epic *Moby-Dick* as an allegory of religiosity, in which the mysterious white whale symbolizes God as something that it is impossible to encapsulate or unambiguously express in human terms. Captain Ahab's hunt for the whale, his desire to capture and contain it, represents his obsession with finding the ultimate truth. As such, Ahab is a fundamentalist – as such, he must perish.

If we return once again to William James' understanding of religion as a person's total reaction upon life, then we can say that faith in either the Christian God or the many gods is ultimately about finding the source of meaning and value in something other than the individual. Faith asserts that there is something in the world that wants something from us, that calls to us. We can open ourselves up to this aspect of life even if we don't fully understand it. I think that if we adopt a less literal approach to religions, we will also find 'gods' (in quotation marks for good order) in art, sport or world history, or in the Anne Frank House – gods that move and inspire us. It will also help us to understand that ideas of love and the good are the foundation of everything we do.

This is essentially the idea I sought to express in my discussions of Plato and Iris Murdoch – that underlying all of our human trials and tribulations is this archaic idea of goodness. As we grow, we develop an awareness of that which comprises the world: nature, culture, history, human communities. Perhaps even the holy, which Nietzsche famously defined as the parts of a culture that it is forbidden to mock[5] – and we certainly can't laugh at Anne Frank's fate. Although I have found it difficult to express what I felt in her house, I think that it would have been even more difficult had I not been able to draw on religious language. Is that not in itself a justification for such language – that it helps us to talk about the world?

September

How does faith affect grief?

10 September

One of the most widely held theories about why humans came up with religion is as a bulwark against our fear of death. The sociologist Clive Seale has even argued that *all* social and cultural life – including our religious practices – is ultimately 'a human construction in the face of death'.[1] Personally, I think about death every day and find it angst-inducing. Although I know that many other people feel the same, I find it difficult to accept the notion that all collective life somehow stems from this – from the idea that we create culture in general, as well as meaning, morality and God, because we are afraid of dying: that it is our recognition of the brevity of life that inspires us to do everything we do.

Along the same lines, another sociologist, Peter Berger, thought that ultimately we should understand society as an assemblage of people united in the face of death. In the 1973 classic *The Denial of Death*, Ernest Becker identified the fear of dying as the single most significant human condition and the main driver of social processes.[2] I could list a host of other philosophers and scientists who have highlighted humanity's fear of death as the primary impetus behind the development of culture and society.

In recent years, I have been part of a research project on 'the culture of grief', as part of which we look at the historical dimension of the phenomenon, and I have also been interested in our relationship with death more generally. I think that there is a great deal of sense in the idea that humankind's unique recognition of the reality of death helps to structure large parts of our existence. When I say 'unique', I don't mean to deny that other living beings, such as monkeys and elephants, seem to have some kind of understanding of death, but it is at best rudimentary and bears no comparison with the human understanding of our mortality. It is a crucial aspect of being human that we know that we are going to die. We know it from childhood, once we have acquired language, usually becoming aware of it when we are about 4.

To date, I have given little thought to the importance of faith and religion in my work on death and grief.[3] I have been influenced by the thinking about death (thanatology is the technical term) handed down from the Stoic philosophers, who preached 'memento mori' (remember, you will die), and twentieth-century existential philosophers such as Heidegger, who argued that being human is a form of being-towards-death. However, as mentioned, I haven't included the importance of religion in my work to any significant extent. In this perspective, thinking about death is about reconciling ourselves with mortality and using it in an edifying way to ensure that we live as well – and as authentically – as possible, albeit without believing in an afterlife or adopting other religious ideas.

As mentioned earlier in this book, I just can't find it in me to believe in an afterlife. I believe that I am identical to the life I live. And that life will end, by definition, when I die. Of course, there is an afterlife in the sense that others live on – but it will not be *my* life. I also believe that the idea of an afterlife is incompatible not only with a scientific world-view but also with the existential fragility of life on which religion is based in so many ways. Reconciling ourselves to this fragility is a daunting enough prospect without bringing metaphysical ideas of an afterlife into the picture. On the other hand, I do fully understand that others find solace in belief in an afterlife. In the face of death, no holds are barred, and it is not for anyone to deprive others of their faith in an afterlife if it brings them comfort during the long, lonely nights.

What I want to do this month is not to reflect on my relationship with my own death or, more generally, the individual's relationship with their own death. The Stoics, Heidegger and many others have already done so quite brilliantly, and there is probably little I could add. I don't know whether there is a gender aspect to this, but I can't help but think that all the great philosophers of death have been men possessed of such huge egos that they were unable to imagine the world without themselves in it. Instead, I want to focus on our human experience of *other people* dying while we live on – in other words, the fact that we as human beings are connected to others who are just as fragile as we are. Very few of the great philosophical egos have made this the focal point of their thinking about life, even though it is a crucial condition for our relationships – that they end with the death of one or the other of us.

It is not just at the moment of death that we ourselves or others die. In a sense, all living beings are dying from the very moment they are born. Grethe Risbjerg Thomsen conveys this in her short poem 'Maybe a March Night' from 1948 (printed in the collection *The Day and The Night*):[4]

I die a little
With every passing second.
I carry death in me
through years of life.

One night, maybe in March,
mild with rain and thaw,
I'll go into the darkness
and stop dying.

We only stop dying when we are no longer alive. This may sound like a paradox, but it serves to illustrate the truth

that life and death are each other's prerequisites. The two
are inextricably interlinked. What acknowledging the death
of *others* may remind us of is not necessarily a thunderous
memento mori, or a *carpe diem* insight into the fact that we
ourselves should live as much as possible – *just do it* before
it's too late! No, it is that we must value the companionship
of other people in our lives because, one day, we will lose
them – unless we die first.

In that sense, life is not only a being-towards-death as
per Heidegger, but also a being-towards-grief, because we
carry the death of others with us 'through years of life',
as Thomsen put it.[5] It may sound melodramatic, but it is
undeniable that we die *together*. The question, then, is what
roles do faith and religion play in this context? Is it even
possible to cope with death without some form of faith? Do
we not have to believe in something – maybe even take part
in religious rituals – to help the drama of life, which ends in
death, to make any kind of sense at all?

11 September

Grief is a universal human experience.[6] Some of the oldest
archaeological finds showing traces of human activity reveal
ceremonies and rituals associated with loss and grief. *Homo
sapiens* have buried their dead for more than 100,000 years.
The phenomenon can be interpreted in many ways – for
example, as a reflection of the fear of their own death among
those who live on – but the most obvious conclusion is that
this is evidence of the human experience of grief. According
to the philosopher Hans Ruin, the ceremonial practices of
loss – and of religion more generally – are closely linked
to the ability to symbolize.[7] Being able to represent others
through symbols after their death seems to be a peculiarly
human characteristic that underpins a host of other symbolic practices. In his poem 'Every year on the date', Søren
Ulrik Thomsen describes the importance of the grave:

Every year on the date
that arbitrarily became your birthday
we take the train to Århus
to visit your grave
which happens to be the place here in the world where
    you are not.
On our way through the city we buy flowers and talk as
    on any other day
until we're standing in front of the stone.
And on the way back it always rains.
Since none of this has meaning
and it takes place anyway
it must be of the greatest significance.[8]

The grave is where the dead are *not*. They are not anywhere else, of course, but a special place is needed to mark their absence. It may well make no sense to visit a place where the dead person is not because your visit will not bring them back, but that's also why it can be of the utmost importance. And this has been the case throughout human history. We have always buried our dead and visited their graves.

In the light of this, it is no great surprise that accounts of human sorrow are as old as the art of writing itself. Think of Gilgamesh's grief for Enkidu, as told in the world's oldest epic poem, or of Achilles' grief over Patroclus in *The Iliad*. Or the Greek tragedies and the countless dramas and novels written ever since. Or some of the contemporary literary offerings that focus on grief. All of them tell us something about the universal experience of loss. They just express it in different ways. Grief is sometimes raw and distressing, as conveyed by Naja Marie Aidt in the book about her son's death.[9] Or it can manifest as an intense confusion, with traits similar to delusions, like those of Joan Didion in the book about her husband.[10] And it can also be portrayed as an extended process of conflicting emotions, as in Linn Ullmann's book about her late father, Ingmar Bergman.[11]

These examples, from recent literature alone, illustrate the range of ways in which grief is felt, even within a relatively homogeneous cultural circle. They are all about the loss of a close relative, as is my own research. But the differences in the ways grief is felt are, of course, even more significant if we take into account the diversity of practices in other eras and cultures. Around the world, there are enormous differences in how long grief is expected to last and the activities, rituals and emotional templates through which it is expressed. In recognition of this great variation, researchers have abandoned old models based on phases of grief that were considered universal and adopted more dynamic understandings – for example, describing grief as a continuous process on two parallel tracks (one loss-oriented, the other restoration-oriented), with ongoing ties to the deceased. These new ways of thinking do not expect us to 'move on' and 'get over' our grief. Instead, they allow us to live with the dead for the rest of our lives. We are not expected to feel deep sorrow all of the time. Of course not. Rather, it just means that we retain our love and attachment to the dead person throughout our lives. Despite the myriad personal and cultural differences in grief, this sense of attachment seems to be a universal phenomenon.

Even if you don't believe in an afterlife, I think that what might be called 'life with the dead' is generally associated with at least a rudimentary form of faith. Grief, more so than any other phenomenon, clearly shows that many of us who do not think of ourselves as religious may actually be so. This can take many forms. For example, we might believe that the dead would have wanted us to live on; or that we now have a responsibility to speak on behalf of those no longer able to speak for themselves. Or it might manifest as gratitude that, when all is said and done, we had the simple privilege of knowing another human being.

None of these ways of living with the dead can be substantiated by science. There's no evidence for them. As such, they suggest a form of faith that may be rooted in defiance – or even seem somewhat absurd. The journalist Charlotte Rørth, for example, says that gratitude was the first thing she felt when her 22-year-old son suddenly committed suicide.[12] She wasn't grateful he was dead, of course, but for the fact that 'we had had him for 22 years'. She writes that she couldn't understand how she could feel such gratitude under the circumstances but insists that this *was* her first emotion. It's conceivable that, in this situation, the feeling might be *explained* scientifically (perhaps as some sort of survival mechanism), but it can't be *justified* by scientific arguments. A genuine understanding of such a seemingly intolerable situation requires more religious or poetic language.

12 September

If human existence is only possible in relation to other people, and if our relationship with others is structured existentially by grief because we know in advance that they will die, then one of the essential characteristics of being human is the ability to grieve. That doesn't mean, of course, that we wander around perpetually aware of our grief. We don't usually grieve when we cook, play football or pick up the kids from school – unless a recent bereavement bears heavily on us. Nonetheless, human life necessarily involves grief. That claim may sound less strange if we take as our starting point the idea that to be human is to exist in relation to others – both living and dead – while maintaining an underlying awareness of the finiteness of these relationships.

As touched on previously, Løgstrup famously wrote that we never have anything to do with another human being without holding some of that person's life in our hand. This is the basis for ethics between the living. My thesis might be explained by adding to Løgstrup's quote: we never hold another's life in our hands without knowing it is finite. One day, we will live to see this person die – unless we die first.

Once the other is dead, we are then responsible for living with them because we hold their whole life story in our hands. From this fact stems the ethical relationship between the living and the dead.

In a similar vein, the philosopher Derrida's thoughts about friendship apply to human relations more generally – that is, they are based on our acknowledging that one of us will die before the other.[13] When one of us is no more, the other is left to take care of the dead person's life. This is the basis of the idea that the human condition can be characterized, in existential terms, as being-towards-grief. I agree with Levinas, therefore, that the acknowledgement of the other's mortality is deeper and existentially more important to me than acknowledging that I will die.[14]

According to the philosopher Hans Jonas – a student of Heidegger who had to leave Germany in 1933 because he was Jewish – the grave is closely linked to our ideas of religion and faith, i.e. the ability to think beyond the sensory, empirical world, since the grave maintains a thread to the absent dead person.[15] Graves can, therefore, be considered the first symbols – or, according to Ruin, even as the oldest form of literature – that bind us to previous generations and remind us that the life we live now is always a life *after*. This is also the grave's message to us. We all always live after someone who came before us. As Ruin puts it, we never overcome the finiteness of death, but 'we share it with the living to which we give birth and for which we too will one day belong to those having-been'.[16]

The web of human life and communities is spun from a thread across generations that links the dead with the living and the as-yet-unborn. To exist as part of history is, therefore, to *live with the dead*. We share the world not only with the living but also with the dead. Again, this means that grief is part of being human. If that is the case, then some kind of religious faith seems indispensable to us (even to atheists) because living with the dead, taking the legacy and desires of the dead seriously, is ultimately based on the understanding that transcends the ordinary empirical world.

A scene in the science-fiction film *Contact* (about human contact with aliens) helps illustrate the point. Jodie Foster plays Ellie, a scientist who denies God's existence because she believes only in what can be proven. Ellie has lost her much loved father, and in one scene, she discusses God's existence with Palmer, a philosopher and man of faith, played by Matthew McConaughey:

> **Ellie:** So what's more likely? That an all-powerful, mysterious God created the Universe, and decided not to give any proof of his existence? Or that He simply doesn't exist at all, and that we created Him, so that we wouldn't have to feel so small and alone?
>
> **Palmer:** I don't know. I couldn't imagine living in a world where God doesn't exist. I wouldn't want to.
>
> **Ellie:** How do you know you're not deluding yourself? I mean, for me, I'd need proof.
>
> **Palmer:** Proof . . . Did you love your father?
>
> **Ellie:** What?
>
> **Palmer:** Your dad. Did you love him?
>
> **Ellie:** Yes, very much.
>
> **Palmer:** Prove it.

She can't, of course. And yet love of her father is a fundamental aspect of her life and persists after his death. We live not only for empirically proven scientific truths, no matter how important they are, but for love, commitment and relationships – even ones that transcend the boundaries between life and death. If the concept of faith is to have any meaning at all in our lives, I think this is where it is most appropriate to use it.

13 September

The ideas outlined over the last few days hopefully convey the idea that grief is an integral part of human life, and that a language of faith is not only relevant for comprehending that dimension but perhaps even essential. We need to be able to talk about it and about those who are no longer with us. Our relationships with others, both living and dead, make us who we are – but these relationships are either already broken (with the dead) or doomed to be so one day (with the living). For this reason, I too am, in a sense, condemned to be 'broken'. This also implies that human grief is impossible because it is not something we can do, order or fix. To the extent that grief about the finiteness of relationships defines me as an individual, my identity is, in a sense, impossible. I know that these concepts seem difficult, but, in a way, they are simple: I am only something by virtue of others, and they are already in the process of dying. I can, therefore, never be whole or complete.

This is also the conclusion reached by the contemporary philosopher Simon Critchley, much of whose writing revolves around death. He writes that the death of a loved one puts us in a position of 'radical impossibility'.[17] It is an event over which we have no control. It is impossible to *will* the other's death away, even if we *wanted* to. It is not a question of motivation or will. We just can't do it. There is nothing we can do, and the grief we feel invades and structures our lives. Critchley believes that humans are ultimately defined by our ability to grieve, as it shows that we can never fully master life but are doomed to fall short due to our dependence on others – others who leave us behind, which renders us existentially impotent and powerless.

According to Critchley, this impotence, as a fundamental form of fragility, is also the source of the ethical demand in our interactions with others. In this sense, grief is linked not only to the belief that the other is worth loving despite their mortality, but also to ethical life in general. The realization that our relationship with the other will end is also the basis for the realization that we spend our entire life holding part of the other's life in our hand – and must take this seriously because that other life will not last forever. In this way, grief becomes the basis for the demand that we provide *care*.

To sum up: I have concluded that grief is impossible because it is directed at a loss that, in principle, is irreversible. Yes, of course, *psychologically* we can, after some time, start to feel better, and perhaps fall in love again and 'move on'. But in a more *existential* sense, grief is not something we can fix because the break is definitive. To grieve is to live with that break. The break was inevitable even before my birth because my life, by its very nature, entails a life after me. This is an intrinsic part of being human.

Nowhere is the point made more clearly than in the Greek tragedies. In a book about the enduring topicality of these tragedies, Critchley argues that tragedy as a genre reveals to us the transitory, the fragile and that which moves slowly in our lives.[18] Grief is one such slow phenomenon, both in the life of the individual and across the generations. That is why we – in the modern world – can read Greek tragedies and still be moved by them millennia later. Tragedy shows us that the Self is totally dependent on others, and that grief is the source of tragedy in our lives. It is said that there are at least thirteen ancient Greek words for grief. Our relative linguistic poverty in this area may indicate that we are less adept at this impossible art than the Greeks were.

Critchley makes a point of comparing tragedy and philosophy. Both flourished at the same time in ancient Greece, but while philosophy (especially that of Plato and Aristotle) was concerned with ironing out contradictions through logical thinking and dialectic, there is something unresolvable about tragedy – as there is with grief. The tragic drama – especially by the greats of the genre, such as Aeschylus, Sophocles and Euripides, all of whom lived in the fifth century BCE – conveys an experience of moral ambiguity and reveals a world 'only partially intelligible to human agency, where autonomy is necessarily limited by the acknowledgement of dependency'.[19] For a philosopher, ambiguity is a sign of a crisis that must be avoided by reference to a higher truth. However, for a Greek tragedian, the crisis simply reflects human life. Where philosophy is idealistic, tragedy is realistic. Modern psychology is idealistic in the same sense, as it seeks to fix or eliminate people's grief by providing linear models for living through it. But grief and tragedy are not linear phenomena – indeed, they are encounters with our destiny in a way that means any attempt to sidestep it only makes it more set in stone.

Plato didn't want poets in his ideal society because he thought they could only produce versions of reality that paled in comparison with philosophy. However, if Critchley is right, the hierarchy should be reversed: it is tragedy that shows us the nature of reality, while philosophy (and scientific psychology) offer only dazzling but unrealistic images. This is where we find common ground between tragedy and religion. Philosophy may enable us to grasp the world through logical systems, but faith and religion direct us towards that which we cannot comprehend and in relation to which we are impotent. And we need that, even if we don't believe in God or an afterlife. Grief teaches us a crucial lesson: we have to act, live and die within a horizon over which we have no control. All we can do is believe that, despite our mortality, life is worth living. The tragedies usually stem from or end with grief, rendered in an artistic form that is relatable and offers relief to the grief-stricken. In Naja Marie Aidt's book about the death of her son, she quotes from the speech given by Carl's older brother at his funeral:

> Aristotle believed that tragedy after a reversal of fate would inspire fear and compassion in the audience. Compassion for those who do not deserve trouble. Fear, when someone

gets into trouble who, in many ways, is like ourselves. . . . And here is the crux of the tragedy and this entire unfortunate situation. We have compassion for Carl – and we feel fear that we ourselves under certain circumstances could have met the same fate. After the tragedy the audience will leave the theatre feeling humble about their own ability to avoid trouble, and will think twice about looking down on one of their fellow human beings, whose life has ended in a failed situation. I hope that everyone with us today in this room will learn from this tragedy.[20]

The lesson to be learned from tragedy is, I believe, the same one religion can teach us: a sense of humility with regard to our ability to avoid misfortune, and solidarity with those who are suffering. Carl's brother talks about fate and how tragedy makes us think. The Greek tragedies he refers to encapsulate the art of grief, as does Aidt's book, from which these words were taken. Both also show how, in situations of tragedy, our feelings become ambiguous, and how, in our grief, we may feel despair, guilt and rage. In this context, the Greek tragedies offer more profound insight into the nature of grief than any psychological theories. It is my belief that the tragedies speak to a common religious sensibility within us over the centuries and millennia.

I began this month with a rapid run-through of some well-known contemporary books on grief – not written by scientists but by those left behind. Each in its own way illustrates the moral ambiguity and lack of coherence in our experience of tragedy and grief. Grief is the art not of the possible but of the impossible. It is impossible because it can't be fixed, and an art because it demands to be performed. There is no getting around it – amid loss and grief, all we can do is choose to believe that life is worth living. This is where I see a faith dimension in grief. However, there is also a more obviously religious dimension related to what might be called the organization of grief. In February,

I discussed several definitions of religion, including this one from Geertz: 'A religion is a system of symbols which acts to establish powerful, pervasive and long-lasting moods and motivations in men by formulating conceptions of a general order of existence.'[21]

All cultures employ a 'system of symbols' to regulate grief, to make it possible to live with the impossible, to bear the unbearable. Symbols and rituals give form to the pain, allowing us to share it with others and bear it together. Aidt expresses both of these in her book:

> We wish rituals still existed.
> So we make our own rituals.
> Our friends make rituals. . . .
>   *The community as something just as absolute as death.*
>   *The community as the only possibility.*[22]

In almost all non-Western countries, rituals and communities take up much of the social space. Our society has largely abandoned collective recommendations and rituals for grief. It is hard to grieve unless society offers a repertoire of rituals that give shape to our pain and invite us to share it with others.

By way of an afterthought: if grief is an impossible art that is an essential part of being human, this also suggests that being human is itself an impossible art. This might seem like a sad conclusion but is, in reality, quite the opposite. It is precisely because it is impossible to be human that we have reason to forgive ourselves and each other for our inadequacies. There is good reason to show solidarity with the other, as they too are struggling to figure things out, and perhaps they too live in the hope that someone will offer them a modicum of comfort and forgiveness. Symbols and rituals don't help us to overcome grief but to live with it in a human way. Despite the impossibility of this project, we must believe that it is worth being human.

24 September

I just heard from one of my childhood friends that he has lost his younger brother. In recent days, I have been reading a number of scientific studies on whether believers and non-believers feel any different after a loss. I wanted to write about that today, but then I heard my friend's news. His brother was relatively young. He went to see a doctor about a sore stomach but otherwise felt healthy. He died a few days later of what turned out to be an extremely aggressive cancer. Suddenly, my reflections on grief and religion seem like an intellectual luxury.

Hearing about a young person dying far too soon puts many things in perspective. It makes the scientific objectivity that views phenomena from a distance and seeks to calculate the correlation between variables seem utterly sterile, almost like a complete misunderstanding. Our lives don't consist of variables but of phenomena like love, disappointments, loss, dreams, duties and much more. The idea that faith might be comforting in such a tragic situation seems almost like wishful thinking. Of course, if it does offer some consolation, that is most welcome – but even just raising the issue risks riding roughshod over other people's genuine and deep despair, which should probably be allowed to run its course. I could never say to my friend, or anyone else in a state of deep grief, that 'studies have shown that it's actually good to have faith because it helps you cope with grief'. That would be absurd.

25 September

With yesterday's tragic news in the back of my mind, maybe it would be of scientific interest to know whether faith does indeed comfort believers during times of bereavement. What does the research say? Do religious people cope better with loss? The numerous studies conducted on this topic

have been summarized in several meta-analyses or systematic reviews. One such review explicitly explored whether
religious beliefs have an impact on the experience of loss.
It found 32 relevant studies involving more than 5,000
respondents. More than 9 out of 10 studies demonstrated
a positive effect of faith.[23] However, the researchers behind
the review also caution that the methodology and quality of
the studies varied, so further research is needed.

Another review looked at religious beliefs as an independent variable – i.e. the extent to which other phenomena,
such as the ability to cope with grief, differ based on this
variable. It concludes, first, that many people *themselves*
believe that faith is 'an effective means' to counter grief,
and second, that there are 15 relatively good studies that
substantiate this belief.[24] However, the researchers behind
this meta-study conclude that there are so many different
forms of religion and so many kinds of grief that the overall
question of the relationship between them is too general to
be meaningful. Again, they recommend further research.
Mind you, that's almost always what researchers conclude!

More interesting in my eyes is a smaller online survey
based on the philosophical discussion of what faith and
atheism actually are.[25] The philosopher Georges Rey has
developed a position he calls meta-atheism, which says
that people who claim to be religious are usually actually
atheists without realizing it. This is particularly relevant
in terms of loss and grief because, when a loved one dies,
the bereaved grieve equally, whether they are believers or
atheists. From Rey's perspective, believers are meta-atheists
because, in practice, they don't really seem to think the
dead have moved on to a better place, which they surely
would if their religious affiliations were sufficiently deep and
sincere. Whereas earlier in this book I argued that all people
are religious on some level, Rey turns this idea around,
claiming that we are all, in fact, basically atheists – or at
least meta-atheists.

The problem with his argument is that it rests on a claim that Rey fails to substantiate – that believers and non-believers grieve equally – one of the questions posed by the small online study mentioned above. Like other studies, it reveals a small but significant difference, suggesting that, three years after a loss, believers report suffering less intense grief than atheists. Immediately after bereavement, both groups reported equally intense feelings of sadness. Does this mean Rey's thesis about meta-atheism is false? Does faith, in fact, have a comforting effect on the bereaved?

The only study I have come across that has come to the opposite conclusion not only looked at religious convictions as a whole but tried to differentiate between the various different kinds.[26] It turns out that what the researchers call 'negative religious coping' tends to lead those grieving into problematic ways of regulating their emotions. For example, the religious may see their loss as a punishment from God or the work of the Devil. In other words, those with a religious temperament predisposed to humility and gratitude will respond differently from those whose faith manifests in submission and fear. All things being equal, faith is more likely to be a source of comfort and help.

A cautious conclusion to my summary of research into the link between faith and grief is that, for most bereaved people, religious faith *does* seem to offer real help – but it depends on the nature of that faith. And maybe the main point is that having templates, including rituals, for grief, as well as communities of like-minded people, is an advantage that atheist individualists do not have. For those left behind, it is meaningful that there is someone there to support them, and religion can be a way of organizing this support.

Following on from April's studies of the effects of faith, this is an interesting scientific insight, but one that is nevertheless difficult to apply in any practical way. Would anybody consciously take the decision to find faith just to prepare for future loss? Might people attempt to 'vaccinate' themselves against future painful experiences by taking a dose of religion? It sounds unlikely. On the other hand, I can well imagine that the experience of loss can lead those left behind to search for meaning and that, for some people, this will lead to faith. The phenomenon of 'post-traumatic growth' – people feeling that they develop personally after a loss – is well documented. In a major Gallup survey in 2020, almost three out of four Danes reported feeling better after a life crisis, including bereavement.[27] Nobody is suggesting that this is because they all found faith, but it does suggest that some of the phenomena associated with faith, such as gratitude, humility, a sense of wonder and a defiant joy in life, have a greater presence in their lives after a loss.

October

Can humans become God?

26 October

It's been a while since I've had the chance to write about God. Over the last few weeks, I've spent a lot of time thinking about this book and speaking to people about it. I've just not had the time to write. In what remains of October, I hope to make up for that by seeking answers to the question: can humans become God? Imagine if we were able to transcend the limitations of human nature and not have to lose loved ones or die!

According to Christianity, we are created in God's image – *Imago Dei* – a concept that theology has long found challenging to explain. Does it mean God has human traits? That we can recognize His true nature by taking an interest in our fellow human beings? Interesting questions for theologians, but perhaps a little strange in other contexts. In recent times, research into religion has been more concerned with the inverse question: is God created in the human image?

The question is, therefore, whether our conceptions of the divine stem from radicalized versions of our perception of the human. In other words, do religions take existing human traits and exaggerate them to the point where they become superhuman and divine? God is not just intelligent the way people are, but omniscient; not just capable of doing good deeds, but omnibenevolent; not just competent, but omnipotent. In this sense, God can be considered a projection and a scaling up of everything that has basic value in our lives. At least, this is the case in Christianity. In other religious contexts – for example, the Greek or Norse pantheons – the gods also embody less noble traits, such as envy and jealousy.

It is an age-old critique of Christianity that God is merely a projection of human nature. This is sometimes called the anthropological critique of religion and is associated with Ludwig Feuerbach in the nineteenth century in particular. Kierkegaard expert Peter Tudvad, who has personally fluctuated between faith and atheism, finds something valuable in this criticism of religion: 'God is an idealized notion of what humans themselves are. God becomes a mirror image and the religious a mirror image of humankind. The deity, or religion and religiosity, testify to what the human is, hence the anthropological. I think that is a fantastically productive initial assumption because it will not just lead to delusion.'[1]

At first glance, I agree with this. Although the idea that the divine is merely an extension of the human seems to diminish the idea of a grand metaphysical deity as an active force in the universe, I still think (like Tudvad, if I have understood him correctly) that the idea can be edifying. It recasts God as a term for the *absence* of human perfection, which we must accept as a reality, but also as an absence that only makes sense because we understand it as the absence of *something* that is perfect, beautiful and ideal.

We, as human beings, are not God because we are not omnibenevolent. But acknowledging our lack of omnibenevolence nevertheless presupposes an understanding of benevolence as an unfulfillable demand in our lives. The concept of God I have favoured in this book (as far back as March) claims that God *is* this unrealizable demand. It's a bit like Iris Murdoch circling around God as *the good*. From this perspective, I described God as a demand that *insists* rather than *exists*, that demands something from us without any quid pro quo, and in which we must believe in order to live – even if we don't call it God.

Since writing the above, I have read the theologian Johannes Sløk, whose thinking is very much in line with these ideas. In his memoir, *Mig og Godot* (Me and Godot), he refers to himself as 'an atheist at heart', based on atheism's assumptions that God is a figure 'up there' in whom we can believe. Sløk thinks that premise is foolish. He writes: 'The difference between me and my atheist friends is simply that for them it goes without saying that the traditional concept of God is nonsense, while for me it's a challenge and a mystery. God ought to be there, but He isn't, and my starting point is, therefore, God's enigmatic absence.'[2]

God's absence is the basic premise underpinning Sløk's existentialist theology. God is not an eternal being who created everything, but an absence conspicuous by its presence – in other words, its presence *as* absence. This is an understanding that appeals to me because it is compatible with what we know about the universe from physics, biology and other sciences.

But what if humans *could* actually fulfil this otherwise impossible demand, which we might call God? What if we could be much better and more perfect, both in the moral sense and also more generally? What if we could live longer? Even much longer – millions of years, maybe – indeed, forever? What if we could avoid petty feelings of revenge and jealousy, as well as physical imperfections like pain and illness? And what if we didn't have to lose others, which was our focal point last month, but could live happily with them for all eternity? Then we would be gods, and not just absent, insistent ones, but present and undeniably existing deities capable of intervening in what happens in the world and influencing our own eternal lives.

Most people would probably think this sounds absurd. How could such a thing ever be possible? It may sound incredible, but more and more philosophers and futurists are entertaining ideas whereby mere mortals become gods. Perhaps the most famous example is the Israeli historian Yuval Noah Harari, whose book *Sapiens*, about human prehistory, was a global bestseller. He followed it up with *Homo*

Deus about the future of human beings. *Homo Deus* is Latin for 'god man' or 'human-as-god'. The book's basic premise is that history began when humans invented the gods,[3] and that it will end with people becoming gods themselves.

Of course, it's not a history of the universe but of humankind – which, according to Harari, began when we invented the gods. He links being human to our ability to create fiction, symbols and imagined worlds, and religion plays a key role in this. The moment a group of relatively intelligent beings began burying their dead, imagining an afterlife and forming images of gods who monitored their actions and demanded sacrifices, they became what we would term people. Prior to this, there were only intelligent primates. In this way, Harari accepts the broad definitions of religion that I introduced earlier this year, in which religion functions as a kind of social glue that holds communities and societies together and is the foundation of what we call culture. When humanity began to form these kinds of societies based on religious ideas, this was the start of *history* (as opposed to *prehistory*). According to Harari, this (hi)story will end when humans become divine, when they transcend their bond with the mortal body and achieve permanent happiness and long lives – perhaps living forever.

Let me say right away that I consider the idea incredible – literally. It lacks credibility. I don't think humans will ever be immortal. However, what interests me about this is not so much the degree of realism (or lack thereof) but that it is taken seriously at all. Not just by Harari himself – whose international bestseller is based on the idea that, within a matter of centuries, it will be possible to achieve eternal life – but also by countless think-tanks, researchers and institutes that are selling these ideas to companies and nation-states around the world.

The best-known example is Singularity University in California. Originally founded by Ray Kurzweil, among others, the company behind it now receives funding from a number of tech giants, including Google. Its stated goal is to help humanity to achieve eternal life, primarily through the development of 'exponential technologies', e.g. artificial intelligence. Sundar Pichai, CEO of Google, says that artificial intelligence will be a far more significant development than fire and electricity because it will change everything – absolutely everything! And this vision of artificial intelligence is much broader than just computers, encompassing nanotechnology, biotechnology, robotics and integrated systems. As such, it has the potential to affect everything we humans do, can do and might want to do.[4]

In an academic context, the idea of the human-as-god is often linked to the movement known as *transhumanism*, the aim of which is to transcend (hence 'trans') the human. The first paragraph of the original version of the transhumanist declaration reads: 'Humanity will be radically changed by technology in the future. We foresee the feasibility of redesigning the human condition, including such parameters as the inevitability of aging, limitations on human and artificial intellects, unchosen psychology, suffering and our confinement to the planet earth.'[5] These are huge ambitions. If we didn't know that scientists around the world take them seriously, we might mistake these ideas for science fiction.

27 October

There is both a quantitative and a qualitative dimension to the idea of the human-as-god. The first concerns *the duration* of life, which is supposed to increase to infinity. In other words, it is envisaged that we need never die, either because we will be able to repair our biological bodies and replace parts as they wear out, and perhaps have nanorobots clean our bloodstream and the myelin sheaths in our brains – or it may become possible to leave our bodies behind completely when technology reaches a level that allows us to interface with the superintelligence of computers and upload our entire consciousness to a digital cloud. We would not be bound by the internal algorithms of the organism but exist as part of a singularity: an eternal, self-sustaining, artificial intelligence with self-enhancing algorithms.

This is the quantitative dimension of the quest for eternity. By the time our local star burns out, in about 4 billion years, our superintelligent systems will have already colonized other solar systems because, unless they also transcend the laws of physics, they will still need energy. How these systems will prepare for the likely endgame for the universe as a whole – in which all energy is evenly distributed, and the temperature everywhere will drop to around absolute zero (called 'the Big Freeze') – remains to be seen. In such a situation, probably only a 'real' god would be able to save the humans-as-gods.

The qualitative dimension of *Homo Deus* is that living for ever should not entail endless torment or boredom, but eternal *happiness*. If we really could merge with an artificial superintelligence, it would be able to feed us exciting, varied and rich experiences all the time. Not just for a week or two, like at Club La Santa, but for ever! Think *The Matrix*, only with a benevolent superintelligence.[6] Should all this pleasure become boring, the machine could introduce sufficient adversity or tedium to provide some contrast and achieve the best possible net result – in other words, sweet, sweet happiness for all. It would be paradise, not on the other side of the mortal veil but here in our own physical reality. It would be a technological solution to the problems of finiteness – not only that we die, but also that we suffer first. The human-as-god would be above such things.

The theory of intelligent design is occasionally posited as an alternative to evolutionary theory, especially in the US, where it has been a hot political topic in several states. Should schools teach both? Intelligent design is closely related to creationism and asserts that humans, animals and life itself were created by an almighty God, rather than through random evolutionary processes. Among serious scientists, there is a broad consensus that the theory of intelligent design is pseudoscience and that the theory of evolution, on all scientific parameters, is infinitely superior. Although advocates of *Homo Deus* don't agree with intelligent design, in a sense they envisage it as a possibility in the future. When humanity devotes its intelligence to designing an artificial intelligence smarter than humans (which we are probably already doing), this superintelligence will at some point be able to design and develop humans-as-gods, which in a way brings us back to *Imago Dei*. The difference is that, in the future, it will be humans who, through superintelligence, create *themselves* in the image of God. When asked, 'Does God exist?', Ray Kurzweil answers, 'Not yet!'[7] Only with the birth of the human-as-god can God truly begin to exist. In this perspective, intelligent design is a false theory of the origins of humanity. It is very likely that most transhumanists subscribe to the theory of evolution, but intelligent design may in the future *become* an accurate account of the origins of the human-as-god. What a wild idea!

Other more or less fantastical variations on this theme exist, too. One of the more curious is argued by some very serious and influential philosophers, including Nick Bostrom of the University of Oxford, and became particularly well known when it was publicly endorsed by Tesla founder Elon Musk. The theory goes that it is highly likely that we are *already* living in a computer simulation created by a future superintelligence. In other words, that we have already created the human-as-god via a form of post-human superintelligence. The argument is based on the thesis that, if new technology continues to develop at the current pace, there will at some point be enough computational capacity to simulate multiple worlds, complete with simulated people who have subjective experiences – who are able to think, feel and act. In fact, it would be possible to simulate an infinitely vast number of virtual worlds. Since there is only one original world, it is much more likely, mathematically speaking, that we are living in a simulation rather than in the 'real' world.

Bostrom argues that a future superintelligence could run simulations of worlds from human history. So perhaps the world of the 2020s is just a replay of a world from an earlier era, perhaps millions of years ago, which we are now reliving as conscious entities inside a gigantic computer. Or maybe the world of the 2020s has never existed anywhere other than in the simulation, in which case we have no idea what the world looks like outside of the simulation – just as the characters in our video games, if they were sufficiently advanced to have consciousness, would have no concept of our world.

Would humans ever be able to verify whether we live in a simulation? Unless one day the superintelligence chooses to write in the sky, 'Yeah, okay, I admit it, you *are* trapped in a simulation', it seems unlikely. However, the science-fiction genre is adept at presenting such thought experiments in dramatic form. *The Matrix* is a prime example, as is the 2016 HBO series *Westworld*, which adds a new and perhaps more realistic twist.[8] The series takes place in a future Western theme park (Westworld), populated by highly advanced robots who interact with paying guests. You can shoot them, have sex with them or just join in the storylines prepared by the park's designers (incidentally, Anthony Hopkins is excellent in the role of the park's human creator).

These robots are not immediately distinguishable from humans, and clearly feel both pleasure and pain. They have individual personalities and autobiographical memories but are unable to form new memories. They have a form of anterograde amnesia, as the condition is called in human psychology. In other words, for them, each day is a fresh start. Every night, the events of the day are erased from their memory so that, for example, they are not afraid of a guest who has paid to kill them day after day. The next day, their lives start all over again. They are trapped in time because they are trapped in their own locked memories.

I am not going to reveal the storyline's numerous, highly complex layers – including a crucial leap in time – but suffice to say that the drama unfolds as the robots gradually come to the realization that they *are* actually robots. They go through a form of awakening and find out that they are prisoners, not only in Westworld but also in their own minds. As such, the series touches on one of the basic concepts in Western philosophy – Plato's Allegory of the Cave, in which it gradually dawns on the cave dwellers that the world they experience is not the real world but merely its shadow. However, unlike in Plato's allegory, in which the humans are trapped, the humans in Westworld are effectively gods, creating an artificial world of robot prisoners for their own pleasure.

The gradual awakening of the Westworld robots is moving and angst-inducing. The story brings to mind Ernest Becker's famous 1973 book *The Denial of Death*, which is about humanity's realization that we are fragile, mortal beings and our attempts to ignore this fact. Becker coined the term 'creature anxiety' to denote the anxious realization that we are mortal, earthly beings, made of the same substance as plants and stones. His psychoanalytic perspective led him to associate this realization with our digestive and excretory system, via which we literally experience ourselves as matter exchanging matter with our surroundings. As the saying goes, dust to dust.

Becker says that humans are the only animals aware that they are *beings* and, therefore, aware of their limitations *as* animals. The Westworld robots gradually achieve a similar consciousness. For them, this revelation brings fear, but also the possibility of existential freedom. As Kierkegaard noted, freedom and anxiety are intertwined. Westworld is a man-made simulation built to suppress our creature anxiety. It is, in effect, humankind's attempt to turn ourselves into God.

Just as Nietzsche says in his essay 'The madman' that 'God is dead – we have killed him', so too must the human-as-god die in *Westworld*'s final episode, when the robots turn on their creator and kill *Homo Deus*.

We can interpret *Westworld* as an allegory of our experience society, which invites us to constantly relate to images, stories and simulations that create experiences without them necessarily being connected to the external world. This has been one of the main themes of pop culture for decades – and certainly since *The Matrix*. But we can also take it as an important reminder of what makes us human – mortality and our cognisance of it. What makes us the unique individuals that we are *is* our (hi)story. The robots can't be real people precisely because they're trapped in the moment, in what they are experiencing here and now. Humans, on the other hand, live temporally, embedded in history. We are defined not only by our inner experiences but by our actions, and by that of which our experiences are actually experiences.

The robots may well have the experience of having had a past full of events that define them, but in reality, these are just programmed experiences. They aren't real. In a philosophical sense, the *Westworld* series is a defence of the importance of the outer, objective world as something fundamental to our humanity and freedom. The more we focus on the subjective – on our inner experience – and encourage each other to 'live in the moment' and 'seize the day', the more difficult it becomes to establish connections with the real world. It may well be dangerous and terrible, but we must nonetheless deal with reality if we want to be free. *Westworld* teaches us that the meaning we all seek in our lives doesn't consist solely of inner experience but requires that we embrace a collective real world and its history.

28 October

We've jumped from one science-fiction scenario to another over the last couple of days. I hope I'm not the only one who derives intellectual inspiration for reflecting on religion from the worlds of film and television. We started with the idea of a future human-as-god capable of living happily ever after, possibly in a simulation, and ended with the idea of the human being in *Westworld* who becomes a god by creating artificial life for their own amusement. Both scenarios are based on the same assumption: that there is an (inner) experience that may or may not be consistent with an (external) reality. And, if the 'real' world is totally different from the reality we experience, then the extent of that difference is only limited by our imagination.

The imagination can be philosophical (as in Plato's Allegory of the Cave), sceptical (as in Descartes), dystopian (as in *The Matrix*) or utopian (as envisaged by the transhumanists). In each case, however, I think the crucial factor is imagination because the stark distinction between inner experience and outer reality is almost certainly a false one. As many of the great philosophers have sought to show, especially in the twentieth century (e.g. Wittgenstein, Merleau-Ponty and psychologists such as James Gibson), our experience of the world is not purely 'inside our heads'. We live our lives in a way that is directed towards a real world that we experience and influence. We access the world through our senses and actions, precisely because we exist in the world by virtue of our physical being – we are not merely 'copying' it in our heads.

If we take our starting point in realism, as this position is called in philosophy (that we have access to the real world), then imagined simulations and the like seem increasingly absurd. In principle, however, it is still a possibility that the human-as-god will arise in *this* 'real' reality – in the form of physical, sentient beings with agency who will prolong their existence infinitely with the help of various technologies that don't exist yet – but which we can envisage in the future.

Several problems remain, however, including with this whole complex of ideas of *Homo Deus* emerging from the use of nano-, bio- and robotics technologies. The first is that humans-as-gods would not be humans, nor would they be gods. I don't even know what we would call creatures that live *so* long and are *so* happy. Perhaps we should call them jellyfish since there is actually one species – *Turritopsis dohrnii* – which is theoretically immortal. They go through numerous developmental stages, but once they reach sexual maturity, they can revert to an earlier stage, as polyps. In principle, this cycle can continue indefinitely – as long as they avoid being eaten. If such beings have any form of consciousness (which is highly questionable), perhaps it is a kind of indifferent wellbeing, as they drift around in warm tropical waters forever: happy and immortal.

But we're not *Turritopsis dohrnii*. And we might well find their form of existence undesirable. Human life includes happiness and unhappiness, joy and suffering, birth and death. To remove our mortality is to remove everything that makes us human. Everything we fundamentally value has value because it is temporary. Therefore, humans-as-gods are not human beings because they can't experience loss. Conversely, nor are they gods, for the reason that their 'life' would be worldly and present, which is at odds with the analysis of the divine as something absent. God is the act that insists on being performed precisely because it has not been performed. God is a hole in the world that can never be filled by people – not even if they were able to become very old indeed while looking after their wellness at Club La Santa. Such gods would be very strange gods indeed.

29 October

I've loved and read science fiction for most of my life. I still love watching films and TV series that use the genre to explore the theme of human nature and its future. For someone interested in philosophy, this is an arena in which many of the abstract discussions take on a narrative form. The surprising thing about the ideas of *Homo Deus* and the transhumanists is that they almost surpass even the most imaginative science-fiction writers. I find it fascinating, but also rather terrifying, that these concepts are taken so seriously and might perhaps even form the basis for decisions that will have significant consequences for real people around the world. Many of the billions invested in technologies aimed at making humans-as-gods a reality could probably be better spent on helping real people currently trapped in poverty.

For that reason, my answer to this month's question is rather definitive: no, we *can't* become God! If future versions of us really did manage to extend life and happiness in an almost miraculous way, that would not mean that God had manifested in the world. Rather, it would mean that some beings had completely lost touch with reality and considered themselves so important that they simply couldn't bear the thought of their own demise. Seeking immortality is not a divine desire. It is an exceedingly human one. Interestingly, it is perhaps only religious language or something like it that can keep this desire in check. So one argument for retaining such language for discussions about life is that it offers a much needed dose of humility and stops us from elevating ourselves to the status of gods. To do so wouldn't be desirable; it would be quite inhuman.

November

What about doubt?

2 November

It's November already. It's been the strangest year I can
remember, not least because of the global pandemic. COVID
has set the agenda for almost everything, including the US
presidential election tomorrow. Trump looked likely to be
re-elected until the virus triggered mass unemployment and
spiralling death rates. Watching reports from the United
States in recent days has reminded me what a powerful
force religion is in that vast country. Journalists seem to
be constantly interviewing Americans who believe Trump
was chosen by God to save them, voters who embody a very
visible form of Christianity that, to be honest, I find pretty
scary. Many of them appear self-righteous, awestruck and
unwavering – almost ecstatic. They worship Trump like a
saviour, or at least a prophet. They seem to lack any doubt
in either their God or their president.

Watching them, I really understand why the country has
also spawned emphatically anti-religious voices. Take, for
example, Sam Harris, one of the new breed of atheists, who
has persistently called religion deeply harmful. He levels
this charge at Islamic fundamentalism, but also at the fundamentalist form of Christianity preached in the United
States, which is closely interwoven with political movements
like Trump-style conservatism, according to Harris. Studies
show that nearly half of Americans appear to be so fundamentalist in their beliefs that they think Jesus will return
on Judgement Day within the next fifty years. If that's really
how they see the world, then they are coming from a totally

different place from those of us who fear the long-term effects of climate change. Why bother thinking long-term when the apocalypse is imminent? Harris has said that the planet is in a state of emergency because the United States is ruled by religious fundamentalists who oppose more long-lasting forms of sustainability, a point made even more apparent by the election of Trump in 2016.[1]

The born-again form of Christianity practised in parts of the United States doesn't exactly seem wracked with doubt. Of course, I can't completely rule out the possibility that even the most vocal televangelists harbour doubts in private while quietly reflecting on the meaning of life and the existence of God. But in the pulpit and on TV, they sell religion as if it were some kind of miracle cure for all of humankind's problems.

I've seen photographs of Trump in the Oval Office, praying with a big group of Christian leaders. The preachers lay hands on him, and they all close their eyes, deep in collective prayer. For a cultural Christian like me, it's deeply unsettling. Perhaps that just says something about my own prejudices, but they look like a group of people who just *know* they're right. I find it alienating. It's precisely this kind of religious self-righteousness, more than anything else, that makes me fundamentally sceptical about the value of faith. It triggers an almost primitive contrarian urge in me to take up the cudgels and become a staunch secularist and atheist. But that would be just as self-righteous, albeit in a different direction, which is why I've been trying to keep it in check all year, as I have looked at whether faith and religion can be anything other than unquestioning self-righteousness. And the answer is, of course, yes, it can. Indeed, my basic premise has been that an equally firm rejection of everything to do with religion – as represented by Harris – is almost as problematic as fundamentalism. Atheism, too, can be excessively sure of itself and lacking in the spirit of inquiry.[2] Bearing all this in mind, I intend to spend the month looking at doubt – a quality fundamentalists of all shades seem to lack. We may hear positive statements about the 'gift of doubt', but few of us ever delve into what doubts really are and what role they should play in our lives. The trigger was a quote I stumbled across recently from the late actor Peter Ustinov. The Internet is full of more or less (often *less*) insightful one-liners, but this particular one struck me: 'Beliefs are what divide people. Doubt unites them.'

I don't know whether Ustinov actually said this, but I take it to mean that those who have faith will typically defend it and perhaps even evangelize to non-believers. Others may oppose them, possibly spreading a different gospel. It can quickly descend into the type of religious wars that have scarred world history. However, everyone – Christian, Muslim, atheist or whatever – has the capacity for doubt, and this implies a fundamental solidarity with other people who *do not know*. We can believe one thing or the other, but we don't *know*. If faith is different from knowledge (and it is), then there can be no faith without doubt. Sometimes people say they *know* there is a God or an afterlife. I have no idea how such statements are supposed to be understood because, by their very nature, we can't know these things. This year, I have even come to the realization that, if we knew that God existed – because He walked among us – He could not be God. He could be a superhuman being with whom we might be good friends, perhaps. But not God.

This is the great thing about knowledge – even if what we know turns out to be false, we can't doubt it while we think we know it. In other words, knowledge excludes doubt, whereas faith presupposes it. I know, for example, that I was born in 1975. It would be wrong to say that this is something I *believe* – and it would be wrong to say that I have *doubts* about my year of birth. But it could, in principle, be the wrong year. What if, for example, my parents have spent the whole of my life trying to hide the fact that I was adopted, wanted to obscure the details behind my true origins, and the ruse was suddenly revealed. In that case, I would have to say that I previously *believed that I knew* that I was born in 1975. It still wouldn't be correct to say that my date of birth is now something I believe. It's something I *know* and, therefore, I never doubt I was born in 1975. I have no doubt because it is not just something I believe.

It is the other way around with the things we believe. Doubt is an intrinsic part of belief. If, for example, I believe that people have a duty to help others in need, then this gives rise to a certain degree of doubt. Could the idea of the ethical demand and an obligation to our fellow humans just be an illusion planted in us by a quirk of evolutionary history? Could I, in reality, have no such obligations? These are possibilities. Indeed, it's pretty likely that evolution has influenced the way we interact with each other, but I can't live my life on the basis that what I consider fundamental to life is merely an illusion. I believe that I sometimes try to do good deeds for the sake of my fellow human beings, but can I rule out that I really do it because I want others to see me as a good person? No. And, indeed, I do often doubt why I do things. But I still believe good deeds are possible. I can live with the belief that I am required and obliged to help others, whether I like it or not. But that belief can never be knowledge, so it must always be accompanied by doubt. In order to believe, we must have doubts about our beliefs.

4 November

It's not just in relation to faith and religion that doubt has a part to play in life. It also plays an important role, albeit in different ways, in domains as diverse as ethics, politics and science. I particularly like the late Danish biosemiotician Jesper Hoffmeyer's 'most important message' (as he himself called it) to his students, as described in his small book with the thought-provoking title *7 ting vi plejer at tro på* (Doubtful: Seven Things We Used to Believe In). Hoffmeyer said that university education is primarily about learning to tolerate doubt.[3] In fact, he recommended that this should also be a necessary component of our general upbringing. I don't know whether Hoffmeyer thought about the fact that the word gospel means the good message, but, in a way, his most crucial message expresses what we might call a *gospel* of doubt, similar to that shared by many scientists. For scientists, doubt is *the* most crucial attribute. In science, the aim is not to find the definitive truth but to generate knowledge that best explains observable phenomena. The best-substantiated theories are not those that are beyond all doubt – because, in science, no dogma is beyond doubt – but, in fact, those that have been doubted the most!

Karl Popper's mid-twentieth-century theory about the philosophy of science may be a bit too mechanical, but his stroke of genius lay in understanding that science isn't about collecting more and more evidence that a theory is *true*. On the contrary, it's about testing whether theories are *false*. It's called the falsification principle. Popper asserted that what defines a theory as 'scientific' is that it can be formulated as hypotheses and then tested – and, in principle, rejected – through empirical investigation. Valid theories are, therefore, those that survive the greatest number of attempts at falsification. However, the fact that a hypothesis hasn't been falsified yet doesn't mean it won't be at some point.

With faith, the situation is quite different. It would make little sense to conduct tests to see whether God exists or subject a Christian interpretation of existence to the falsification principle. When it comes to religion, we are simply dealing with a completely different category of questions (existential *clarifications*, rather than scientific *explanations*). Nonetheless, doubt is a common component of both science and faith. After all, subjecting your hypotheses and theories to falsification is only possible because of the existence of doubt: could I be proved wrong? If it is possible, at least in principle, then we are dealing with science.

As far as faith is concerned, we may also turn out to be wrong – not through empirical experiments, but existentially, based on whether our faith offers a meaningful and more or less coherent outlook on life. For example, if we say that 'God is love', we are not dealing with a scientific theory that can be translated into a testable hypothesis. Instead, we are dealing with an interpretation of a basic existential condition, which we can never cease relating to or doubting. It may sound corny, but, if you want to believe, you can never stop doubting. The two belong together, like the convex and concave parts of a curved surface – two aspects of the same phenomenon.

I'm not about to pass judgement on how other people deal with their faith, but I'm pretty distrustful of dogmatic preachers. Personally, I would be more drawn to those who proclaim, for example, 'We don't know what God is or whether He even exists. But God is probably the best image we can come up with for love and goodness. Let's try to live our lives in a way that makes that love a reality. We may have doubts about how best to do this, but let's work together and help each other.'

5 November

It was Descartes who revolutionized philosophy in the first half of the seventeenth century by introducing the idea of a methodical approach to doubt. Instead of starting from what people thought was known at the time – for example, that the world had been created by an almighty God – he started from a position of doubt. By methodically doubting all of his convictions, he concluded that all he knew for sure was that he himself existed, hence his famous phrase 'cogito ergo sum' (I think, therefore I am). Descartes was able to doubt everything, from the existence of the outside world (how do I really know that there is something outside my own consciousness?) to the existence of other people (am I the only one who exists?). But, as long as he doubted – and thus thought – he could at least be sure that he himself, the doubter and thinker, existed.

While the basis of the medieval monks' faith was God and Aristotle, Descartes ushered in modern philosophy – and, arguably, modernity as a whole – by starting with the self and the existence of consciousness. From there, he sought to build up certain knowledge and, in doing so, claimed to prove incontrovertibly that God exists. His proof stems from the fact that man is, on the one hand, a mortal and fallible being. On the other hand, we have a 'clear and distinct idea' of an eternal and infallible being. Descartes concluded that this idea could only come from such a being, not from ourselves – hence God must exist. The idea of infinity can only come from an infinite being.

Few people today would accept Descartes's argument, but it is interesting how doubt could lead him to a realization of both his own and God's existence, which he then concluded was incontrovertible. Descartes invented a method of doubt that ultimately led him to certainty. However, I think there is good reason to hold on to doubt a little longer than Descartes himself did, at least if it's true that faith and doubt necessarily go hand in hand. I even think that it is, in a sense, a defining characteristic of humankind that we possess the ability to doubt. Animals have no doubts. They can be hesitant, alert, etc., but we are unlikely to say, 'Look, at that cat on the windowsill, clearly doubting something.' The cat is probably not in doubt because they are not spiritual beings – and doubt and spirit belong together.

As I touched on in July, as far as we know, only humans are spiritual beings. Only humans relate to themselves because only humans can see themselves from the outside. Therefore, only humans can doubt this or that – and, ultimately, the entire basis of their lives. Existential anxiety or doubt only strikes humans – not dogs, not cats, not canaries. I would even go so far as to say that the ability to doubt is an important ethical virtue. That is not to say that we should have constant doubts, but that the very ability to have them is a prerequisite for understanding that other people's outlook on life and interpretation of it can be legitimate. I must be able to doubt the basis of my own life in order to accept that the lives of others can differ from mine. Again, it's doubt, rather than faith, that can unite us despite our differences.

But how do we reconcile the ability to doubt with having faith in something? The philosopher Richard Rorty tackled this problem. He saw raising doubts about the foundation of our lives as an existential ideal. He described it as a kind of existential irony that we should acknowledge that our own particular worldview is just one among many and that, at some point, we will run out of justifications for it. But that doesn't mean we have to shop around for a new one. Instead, we stand firm on the view of the world we have, accepting all the while that other people have different perspectives and experiences. This is the nature of tolerance.

Hannah Arendt, the German philosopher whom I have mentioned several times, expressed the fundamental value of doubt as follows, in her famous book on the human condition: 'Even if there is no truth, man can be truthful, and even if there is no reliable certainty, man can be reliable.'[4] I really like this quote, which, incidentally, stems from Arendt discussing Cartesian doubt. The point of the quote is that, even if we never reach a single definitive truth about the world – for example, if we never determine whether there is a God or any grand, underlying truth – this is no excuse for being dishonest or unreliable. Speaking the truth and striving to be someone upon whom others can count are universal virtues, no matter what we might otherwise believe in, and regardless of the circumstances in which we find ourselves. According to the concept of God that I have been exploring in this book, it is precisely the absence of truth and reliable certainty that demands that we strive to be truthful and reliable.

As discussed earlier, God can be considered a term denoting an absence in the world – one humans are required to remedy to the best of their ability. As such, my answer to the question of doubt and faith is that we must celebrate and embrace doubt because that is the only way to guard against the illusion that we *know* about existential matters. It is also the only way to avoid zealous fundamentalism. Paradoxically, embracing doubt also presupposes that we sometimes have doubts about doubt itself. It's not always welcome in every context. If you think it's a good thing constantly to doubt the love of those dearest to you, for example, then I think perhaps you've not quite grasped the concept.

6 November

One question still troubles me: how do we prevent doubt from descending into despair? After all, doubting the entire foundation of life could quickly lead to the angst-inducing realization that everything is arbitrary. If I were born in another place, at another time, I'd probably be a completely different person now, with completely different thoughts and beliefs. Does that mean nothing is truer than anything else, and therefore it doesn't matter what you think or believe?

More than any other, that is the approach to life I most wish to challenge. There *are* some things that are more true than others – even if, as limited beings, we can never arrive at the complete truth about life, the universe and everything (as the comic science-fiction author Douglas Adams put it). Our beliefs and values matter. The world isn't a blank canvas on which we can project whatever we want. It is full of meaning and significance that we are born into and invited to explore. What Rosa called resonance is an important aspect of experiencing the world as a meaningful place. Resonance is the antidote to the despair that arises from lack of meaning – and, more importantly, it is totally compatible with doubt. Doubt and despair are *not* the same. Quite the contrary.

Søren Kierkegaard produced the most thorough analysis of the forms of despair in *The Sickness unto Death*.[5] He defined despair as a sickness of the Self – a spiritual malaise. When the self-relating relationship that constitutes the Self lacks harmony, it leads to despair. According to Kierkegaard, despair comes in three forms: despair at not being conscious of having a self; despair at not wanting to be yourself; and despair at wanting to be yourself. I think despair also arises when we lose all sense of meaning. As mentioned previously, Kierkegaard defines spirit as the Self. As such, if we are not conscious of having a Self, or if we experience despair at wanting or not wanting to be that Self, it means that we lack an awareness of spirit, which in this context is synonymous with meaning. Despair, therefore, arises from the loss of meaning. But despair is quite different from doubt, which is not necessarily about meaning but is concerned with much more specific questions. The opposite of faith is not doubt. Indeed, as I have argued, the two are inextricably linked. The opposite of faith is the despair that there is nothing in which it is worth having faith. It's a form of nihilism, which is, in my opinion, the biggest problem facing modern humankind.

I'm acutely aware that these are complex issues, so let me attempt to sum up. If we believe that there is no spirit or meaning, no value and no purpose whatsoever, then we are in despair. If faith and doubt are linked (like the convex surface and the concave one mentioned previously), then we can actually say that doubt is a cure for despair because doubt implies that there really *is* something to believe in – and vice versa. If there's nothing to believe in, there's nothing to doubt! Doubt, therefore, presupposes meaning, whereas despair stems from a lack of meaning. Doubt alone can never, therefore, lead to despair. But if we never acquire the capacity for doubt, we run the risk of succumbing to despair when, for example, we realize that our outlook on life is arbitrary or unjustifiable. For example, if a person who has spent their life believing in an omnibenevolent God, without doubting their belief for a moment, suffers a terrible tragedy, they risk being plunged into deep despair should they also lose their faith in God, without which they see no point in anything. I believe it's important, at a very fundamental level, to learn to doubt – not just in order to be critical of faith, but because it is an essential prerequisite for the capacity to believe.

7 November

The recent days spent with doubt, or rather thinking *about* doubt, very quickly led me to the fairly obvious conclusion that faith and doubt are linked. I've referred several times to William James, one of the founders of American psychology. It was he who took an interest in religion as our 'total reaction upon life'. He also wrote about faith and 'the will to believe' – that it can be rational to believe even when there is a lack of evidence to substantiate our faith. According to James, this applies to religious faith, but there are many human spheres in which life is enhanced by the will to believe. For example, if we believe that the students we teach will actually learn something, then they are much more likely to do so. If we approach other people in the belief that they are trustworthy, they are probably more likely to be reliable than if we approach them with suspicion. This is called the Pygmalion effect and describes a kind of self-fulfilling prophecy. Various studies have documented this phenomenon – and it works both ways, both positively and negatively.

However, the will to believe must also be accompanied by a willingness to doubt. Because sometimes, things don't go the way we want. We sometimes feel let down. The world sometimes changes. Others sometimes think differently from us. In such cases, doubt about our own view of the world can be a good thing, as long as it doesn't descend into despair. But that only happens if we abandon doubt entirely in favour of a dogmatic self-assuredness that leaves us vulnerable to total meltdown. If we stake everything on one particular worldview, the foundations of which are shaken, then despair is close at hand. If we instead cultivate a more humble and curious sense of faith/doubt – in which the two are mutually interlinked – we will be able to engage in edifying interactions with the world and with other people. However, as Hoffmeyer pointed out, a prerequisite for this is that we have been actively taught to tolerate doubt. Just as there are courses in critical thinking and scientific methodology, perhaps our educational institutions should also offer courses in doubt so that no one ends up trapped in rigid dogma that leads to despair.

December

What have I learnt?

18 December

The Christmas season is upon us. So, unfortunately, is a pretty severe lockdown. The pandemic and soaring infection rates have prompted the government to close shopping centres, hairdressers and gyms. Were it not for the fact that the first vaccines will be administered between Christmas and New Year, the sense of hopelessness would probably be palpable. Although large numbers of people are infected, and in hospital, the prospect of the vaccine offers a legitimate hope that life may return to some semblance of normality next year.

Everybody seems to be saying that 2020 has been the strangest year in living memory. It probably has. It's been awful. COVID-19 has brought illness, anxiety and loneliness, not to mention bankruptcy and unemployment. But for me personally, the fact that all sorts of events have been called off has left me with more time than expected to spend on this book. Back in January, I didn't really know whether it was going to work. But here I am, with a full-length manuscript, and satisfied with the quantity of my writing. The big question is: what about the quality? That's a bit more difficult to answer.

As a prelude to this final month, in which I will take stock of my year with God, I've reread the whole thing. I note that the book has become a curious mix of scientific and philosophical discussions of concepts and contexts – drawing on both theology and psychology – as well as more personal and existential considerations. It's probably the most unusual book I've ever written, and I worry that I'm going to fall out with everybody. My humanist friends (of whom there are many), who celebrate Enlightenment ideals and consider religion in all its forms to be nothing but superstition, may think I've sold out by entering the sphere of religion. Why waste time on such nonsense? Conversely, my theologically savvy friends (of whom there are also many) may well accuse me of pure dilettantism. Why not leave religion to those better qualified to discuss it?

To the first group, I would respond that I can't imagine a more wonderful waste of time than reflecting on the microscopic scale of humankind in the vastness of the universe, the fragile nature of unconditionality in an instrumentalized world, or questions of faith, loss and forgiveness. Does any of it serve a purpose? Maybe not, in a pragmatic sense, and it probably adds little to my CV that I've spent a year thinking about such abstract matters, but I still maintain that this kind of contemplation is a fundamentally human endeavour. In fact, in my view, it is a commendable pursuit, irrespective of whether you reach the same conclusions as me.

To the second group – the theologians – I would say: 'Guilty as charged'. There's no escaping the fact that I'm a dilettante when it comes to theology. But I have at least striven for existential sincerity. Each month, I have thought through the questions to the best of my ability – I didn't start out with the conclusions and work backwards. As a researcher by trade, I also have a certain training in reading scientific studies and evaluating philosophical reasoning, and I've sought to bring this experience to bear. As such, despite being an amateur when it comes to theology, I still hope that my reflections will provide food for thought for you, the reader – whether you are· a believer or not. The point has never been to encourage you to draw the same conclusions as me, but it's vital that we all ask these questions.

I hope the book amounts to more than just my own personal voyage of discovery. Hopefully, it will serve as a more general exploration of whether faith and religion still have a role to play for scientifically minded types in a secularized culture.

21 December

So, do faith and religion have roles to play in life today? What conclusions have I drawn? At the risk of this becoming too much like a school assignment, I will try to answer briefly and simply the eleven questions that have guided me through my year with God.

Why a book about God? For one thing, this is a subject of general human interest. One of the unique features of humanity is that we are capable of asking the really big questions – about creation and death, time and eternity. On a personal level, I have sought to fill a gap in both my thinking and my books when it comes to religion.

What is religion? First of all, religion is different from faith. Faith is a personal matter, while religion is a collective practice. Religion binds members of communities together, especially through shared rituals, and facilitates the construction of what we call society. I have discovered that in my own life; I have encountered religion in many forms without thinking of them as religious. I've also experienced religion and faith as resonances that reveal my 'total reaction upon life' and the world, as it were.

Is there a link between ethics and faith? The answer to this question depends on how you define the concepts. I consider it risky to attach a specific form of ethics to a particular religious belief. To do so is to risk a rapid descent into fundamentalism. I agree with Løgstrup, who, despite his Christianity, famously rejected the possibility of specifically Christian ethics. He thought there are only human ethics, but added that people's relationships with God are determined by their relationships with each other. However, if we instead interpret faith in the good (the unconditional) as an expression of a religious belief, then the answer is yes – ethics and faith are indeed connected. As such, any belief in the value of the unconditional constitutes a kind of religious outlook on life since it can't be scientifically proven, no matter how inescapable it may be.

Does faith work? The short answer seems to be yes. It's an incontestable fact that religions have triggered war and oppression, but it also appears that personal faith has beneficial effects on individual happiness, health and longevity. Nevertheless, I think it is problematic to let these kinds of positive effects determine whether or not we believe, because to do so risks turning faith into a kind of quid pro quo, against which I have consistently argued. As soon as you set conditions for the unconditional, you negate its unconditionality!

Can science replace religion? Not directly, because science is concerned with *explanations*, while religion seeks *clarifications*. In short, they deal with different things. What we can do is infer religious implications from science – what Neil deGrasse Tyson calls a 'cosmic perspective', nurtured through astrophysics, cosmology and the theory of evolution. This perspective inspires humility and wonder and encourages people to reflect on their smallness and how they act in this world. That, in turn, raises questions of faith. But we mustn't conflate science and religion, as do, for example, the creationists with their contention that religious tracts can compete with scientific explanations of the world.

Does the soul exist? Not as an object in the world, but probably as a necessary attitude to our fellow human beings. Just as God doesn't have to exist as a powerful creature in our world, but can simply be the name of the insistence with which we are confronted because we live in a world with other people, so the soul doesn't need to be anything other than an insistence on treating others well. The soul doesn't show up on brain scans because it isn't in the brain. The soul isn't a *thing*, but it's not *nothing* either. It is linked to the dignity of the lives we live.

What can we learn from the Bible? This question is almost impossible to answer, as the Bible and its reception history have helped to shape almost our entire culture. From my academic perspective in psychology and philosophy, I have confined myself to three observations: the Bible teaches us about the genesis of humans as spiritual beings; about ethics as an unconditional demand; and about the complexity of human life, in which not everything can be reduced to a mathematical equation. I could have mentioned myriad other insights, but that would take too long – and, besides, I am not sufficiently well versed in the Bible.

Could there be multiple gods? For Christians, the very idea is a heresy. But we can talk about gods – for want of a better word – as a reflection of the moods that seize and move us. The Greeks knew that humankind doesn't inhabit a world devoid of meaning and value, in which the individual is the originator of all decisions. We need religious language in order to understand that there is something in the world that 'calls' us and 'moves' us. This language doesn't have to refer specifically to 'gods', but we must be able to experience and comprehend the resonance that arises when we engage with a living, responsive world – one that is far more than just an echo chamber for our own voices.

How does faith affect grief? We must keep believing that life is worth living despite being destined to lose those we hold dear. It is a universally human trait that we take care of the dead and honour their legacy and last wishes. We owe the dead something because we are still alive to speak for them. This understanding is based on a faith that most people share and which all cultures organize as rituals and practices that, almost by definition, have a religious element. Is it excessive to say that anyone who believes that life doesn't start over from scratch for every new generation has religious faith? Perhaps. But I don't know how else to express a view on this fundamental aspect of being human.

Can humans become God? No. But some people think we can. If a human being did become inviolable and immortal, they might be akin to Superman but not God. *Homo Deus* is really just *Homo Super*. And God isn't super; God is an absence from our world that we can never fully remedy, but which nonetheless demands that we attempt to do so. The dream of eternal life free from suffering is our dream of a return to paradise. But, in that paradise, we would be neither gods nor humans. We would be more like animals, lacking any concept of eternity. I have suggested that a particular species of jellyfish is the closest any living creature has come to this state, so, ultimately, there is still value in being human, despite the brevity and problematic nature of our lives.

What about doubt? In short, there can be no faith without doubt. The two are conceptual twins, and I believe that all of us should be trained to understand and use the concept. We should hold evening classes in doubt. The alternative is fundamentalism, doctrinaire thinking and excessive confidence in your beliefs. A similar attitude is also evident in more general, non-religious existential discussions, especially when people throw themselves wholeheartedly into conspiracy theories. If this book can help the reader, even in small ways, to foster and embrace their doubt, it will have done its job. This is certainly something I myself have sought to develop this year. And, in doing so, the lesson I have learnt is that doubt and faith go hand in hand.

22 December

My exploration of faith over the past year began with the question I asked myself as a child: does God exist? If there's a God, it would change everything. And that makes it one of the most important questions a human being can ask – maybe the most important of all.

Anyone who reflects on the questions I raise in this book will end up with their own specific answers. In a secularized culture, we shouldn't ram religion down anyone's throat, and many will probably refuse to accept the concept of God that I have put forward. Namely, that God is absent and that we know Him as an absence, as a demand that must be met, even if fulfilling that demand is impossible – and even if it weren't impossible, there would be no prizes for fulfilling it anyway.

Many will object that this is a very strange idea of God. And that's fine. I reckon that many others are just as averse as I am to religious proselytizing, so the point isn't that readers should arrive at exactly the same answers as me. But I would insist that we remain curious, that we ask questions that go beyond the ones that science is capable of explaining. We also need existential clarification. In this endeavour, we are not alone, acting in isolation. Humanity has always pondered such matters, so no one is starting from scratch – even if it may sometimes seem that way in our individualized age focused on authenticity. We have priests, philosophers, artists and many others to help us, because they speak a language conducive to considering matters of faith and spirit. As the historian of ideas Hans-Jørgen Schanz writes in his book about spirit:

> Poetic language and religious language are under pressure like never before. Here, in these special languages there was, of course, room for the spirit. One consequence of this is that we lack language for a number of phenomena and manifestations of life in which a scientific vocabulary fits like a shoe on a hand. Not least when it comes to people's feelings and sensory perceptions and, to a large extent, human existential conditions.[1]

We lack a language for all of the matters I have tried to discuss in this book. If we simply use the explanatory language of science, the phenomenon of religion is reduced to a concrete absurdity. As the famous (anti-)psychiatrist Thomas Szasz put it: 'If you talk to God, you are praying; if God talks to you, you have schizophrenia.' He was criticizing the scientific reduction of religious experience to psychotic symptoms. I agree that this kind of pathologization deserves criticism, even if the religiosity I have unfolded in this book is not an 'experiential religiosity' – in fact, quite the contrary (here, my upbringing in a Protestant culture undoubtedly plays a major role). This is not because I want to downplay people's religious experiences. Rather, I believe that religion is primarily linked to our lives, actions and attitudes towards the world and other people. I don't think there is a special category of experience that is exclusively religious.

One of the key takeaways this year has been that we need the language of poetry and religion in order to comprehend life. If it makes sense to talk about religious truth, then it must be poetic. As Søren Ulrik Thomsen writes: 'Death I can't possibly imagine, but the resurrection could well be the sound of a polished little bicycle bell somewhere out there in the morning darkness.'[2] Literally speaking, it makes little sense that the resurrection should be the sound of a bicycle bell, but it directs our attention to the remarkable fact that the world not only exists but continues to do so. The bicycle bell is a minuscule object in an enormous world, but it can still be the starting point for some kind of experience of totality (for want of a better term) – in other words, a sense of wonder at everything. In her book on the life of the mind, Hannah Arendt quotes a splendid passage from the poet Coleridge, who lived a few hundred years ago and, of course, articulated himself in a way that sounds pathos-filled today, and also pointed to this experience of totality:

Hast thou ever raised thy mind to the consideration of existence, in and by itself, as the mere act of existing? Hast though ever said to thyself thoughtfully: It is! Heedless in that moment, whether it were a man before thee, or a flower, or a grain of sand – without reference, in short, to this or that particular mode or form of existence? If thou hast indeed attained to this, thou wilt have felt the presence of a mystery, which must have fixed thy spirit in awe and wonder. . . . If thou hast mastered this intuition of absolute existence, thou wilt have learned likewise that it was this and no other, which in the earlier ages seized the nobler minds, the elect among men, with a sort of sacred horror. This it was that first caused them to feel within themselves a something ineffably greater than their own individual nature.[3]

What Coleridge describes above is a condensed form of total relationship with the world. This is, perhaps more than anything, what a religious sensibility offers. While considering existence, in and of itself, may give rise to what Coleridge calls 'a sort of sacred horror', I would say that it can also give rise to a sense of belonging in the world. Very broadly speaking, we might say that psychology helps us to study other people and be among them (e.g. in a family); the social sciences illuminate what it means to belong to a society with others; and religion thematizes our belonging to the world in general. This may involve a belief in a personal god, a plurality of gods, mystical energies, nature or simply that life is worth living despite defeat, pain and death. Psychology orients us to ourselves and our relationships; politics orients us to society; and religion orients us to the world as a whole – with or without God.

23 December

In addition to this three-tiered belonging – among people, in a society, and to the world as a whole – another major distinction is the one outlined by Kierkegaard between the aesthetic, the ethical and the religious. Here, there is some overlap with yesterday's reflections, but Kierkegaard perhaps draws the boundaries more precisely. One of my major concerns during this project has been the relationship between the aesthetic (the immediate and what we experience) and the ethical (commitment and the general), and I have sought to make a case for the profound importance of ethics in our lives. It might be said that aesthetics is about our relationship to objects, situations and events – specifically, that we want them to be beautiful, moving or entertaining. Ethics is about our relationship with other people. By reducing them to something that can be seen through the same lens as aesthetics, we turn them into objects. Ethics is about dignity and responsibility, which we can't understand in aesthetic terms. I have defended this way of thinking.

Religion has both aesthetic and ethical aspects, of course, in that it often involves both experiences and ethics. However, in this book, I have arrived at an understanding of religion that relates to our relationship with the world as a whole – something that neither the aesthetic nor the ethical does directly. It is the preserve of the religious dimension. If we are unable to discuss this relationship with each other, we lack an elementary part of what makes us human. It would render us incapable of having a dialogue with voices of the past – in a Christian context, with Jesus, Augustine, Aquinas, Luther, etc., but also with all sorts of voices from other religions – because we would no longer be able to understand their views.

In his famous last interview (with *Der Spiegel*), printed after his death in 1976, Heidegger stated that 'Only a god can save us now.' In an era that Heidegger saw as blighted by instrumentalization and the reduction of everything to resources and utilitarian value, we need to ask questions other than those rooted in science and technology and their ways of thinking. In many ways, I agree with Heidegger's critique of culture, but, at the same time, I have tried to argue that, paradoxically, our salvation lies in the very absence of a god capable of saving us. Since god is notable by being absent in a secularized world, it is up to all of us, individually and collectively, to live as well as possible and be there for each other.

I find this acknowledgement clearly expressed in Christianity – mainly in the teachings of Jesus, but also, to a lesser extent, in the traditions of the Christian Church. (Others who are more knowledgeable than I must discuss whether other religious contexts have something similar.) In a world that is sometimes overwhelming and chaotic, religion is one of the few stabilizing elements that connects us to culture and the past and transcends instrumental logic. We need to live in a world that responds to us, that is rich in meaning and value, and that we feel obliged to care for in ways that go beyond our own small lives. I find it hard to see how this would be possible without embracing the language of faith and religion.

And so, my year with God draws to a close. On my 45th birthday. It seems appropriate. Tomorrow is Christmas Eve, and I will join my immediate family to celebrate the birth of Jesus, which also coincides with ancient pagan midwinter feasts. Without lapsing into the overly sentimental, it is a moment of profound resonance every year, as we sing hymns, think about the passing of time, and send kind thoughts to those no longer with us.

I can't say that I've become religious this year. But I have discovered that, in several ways, I've always been religious. I think I'll keep describing myself as 'agnostic' on Facebook, though. Not because I would find it embarrassing to edit my profile, but because the concept actually expresses my standpoint quite accurately. Agnosticism is a kind of faith for doubters. We don't know if there's a God. And precisely because nobody can prove the existence of God – of the unconditional – it is up to us to tell stories about those who have embodied the unconditional. In Christianity, it is

Jesus. If we lose faith in the unconditional, all we have left are the logics of instrumentalization, opportunism and the shopkeeper. While these are perfectly sound on their own terms, they are a very feeble basis for an outlook on life. Or for life in general.

Notes

Preface

1 According to the Pew Research Center, the figure for those who profess no faith at all may be as low as 16 per cent of the global population: www.pewforum.org/2012/12/18/global-religious-landscape-exec.

January

1 P. Qvortrup (2019). *Ind i en stjerne* (Into a Star). Copenhagen: Grif, p. 28.
2 T. Holland (2019). *Dominion: How the Christian Revolution Remade the World*. New York: Basic Books.
3 C. Taylor (2007). *A Secular Age*. Cambridge, MA: Harvard University Press.
4 R. N. Goldstein (2010). *36 Arguments for the Existence of God: A Work of Fiction*. New York: Vintage Books.
5 From Wittgenstein's 'Vortrag über die Ethik und andere kleine Schriften', cited here from Ludwig Wittgenstein (2014). *Lecture on Ethics*, ed. Edoardo Zamuner, Ermelinda Valantina Di Lascio and D. K. Levy. Aarhus: John Wiley & Sons, Inc., p. 47.

February

1 H. Rosa (2019). *Resonance: A Sociology of Our Relationship to the World*. Cambridge: Polity.
2 Rosa, *Resonance*, p. 258.
3 C. Taylor (2007). *A Secular Age*. Cambridge, MA: Harvard University Press, p. 347.

4 www.folkeskolen.dk/646479/professor-i-religionsvidenskab -religion-har-ikke-noget-med-tro-at-goere.

5 H. Ruin (2018). *Being with the Dead: Burial, Ancestral Politics, and the Roots of Historical Consciousness.* Stanford University Press.

6 S. Brinkmann (2007). Det nye præsteskab – Religion som Ritalin for folket! In J. Haviv (ed.). *Medarbejder eller modarbejder – Religion i moderne arbejdsliv.* Aarhus: Klim.

7 Armin W. Geertz and Jeppe Sinding Jensen (2011). *Religious Narrative, Cognition and Culture: Image and Word in the Mind of Narrative.* New York: Routledge, p. 9.

8 B. Turner (1991). *Religion and Social Theory* (2nd edn). London: Sage, p. xi.

9 R. Bellah (2011). *Religion in Human Evolution: From the Paleolithic to the Axial Age.* Cambridge, MA: Harvard University Press.

10 Clifford Geertz (1966). *Religion as a Cultural System.* London: Tavistock, p. 4.

March

1 I. Murdoch (1997). The sovereignty of good over other concepts [1967]. In P. Conradi (ed.), *Existentialists and Mystics: Writings of Philosophy and Literature.* London: Penguin.

2 Plato (2009). *Samlede værker i ny oversættelse I.* Copenhagen: Gyldendal.

3 S. M. Cohen (1971). Socrates on the definition of piety: Euthyphro 10A–11B. *Journal of the History of Philosophy* 9(1), p. 2.

4 I. Murdoch (1997). On 'God' and 'good' [1969]. In Conradi (ed.), *Existentialists and Mystics.*

5 I have expanded on the following in greater depth in S. Brinkmann, *Standpoints: 10 Old Ideas in a New World* [originally in Danish, 2016]. Cambridge: Polity, 2018.

6 K. E. Løgstrup (1991). *Den etiske fordring.* [1956]. Copenhagen: Samlerens Bogklub.

7   Murdoch, On 'God' and 'good', p. 344.
8   I have written about this in greater depth in *Standpoints*.
9   Murdoch, On 'God' and 'good', p. 353.
10   Murdoch, On 'God' and 'good', p. 361.
11   J. Caputo (2016). *The Folly of God: A Theology of the Unconditional*. Salem: Polebridge Press.
12   https://biblehub.com/p/kjv/esv/1_corinthians/1.shtml.
13   Caputo, *The Folly of God*, p. 124.
14   Caputo, *The Folly of God*, p. 122.
15   Caputo, *The Folly of God*, p. 74.
16   E. Carrère (2017). *The Kingdom* [originally in French, 2014], trans. John Lambert. New York: Farrar, Straus and Giroux, p. 368.
17   F. Nietzsche (1977). *The Portable Nietzsche*, ed. and trans. Walter Kaufmann. London: London Bridge Books, p. 95.
18   Caputo, *The Folly of God*, p. 109.

April

1   M. Houellebecq (2001). *Atomised*. London: Vintage.
2   An easily accessible source is: www.lrb.co.uk/the-paper/v21/n06/slavoj-zizek/you-may!
3   A. Ehrenberg (2009). *The Weariness of the Self: Diagnosing the History of Depression in the Contemporary Age*. Montreal: McGill-Queen's University Press.
4   M. E. P. Seligman (2002). *Authentic Happiness: Using the New Positive Psychology to Realize Your Potential for Lasting Fulfillment*. London: Nicholas Brealey Publishing, p. 61.
5   S. Brinkmann (2017). *Stand Firm: Resisting the Self-Improvement Craze*. Cambridge: Polity.
6   C. A. Lewis and S. M. Cruise (2006). Religion and happiness: consensus, contradictions, comments and concerns. *Mental Health, Religion & Culture*, 9, pp. 213–25.
7   E. Diener, L. Tay and D. G. Myers (2011). The religion paradox: if religion makes people happy, why are so many

dropping out? *Journal of Personality and Social Psychology* 101, pp. 1278–90.

8 Diener et al., The religion paradox, p. 1278.

9 P. Bruckner (2010). *Perpetual Euphoria: On the Duty to Be Happy*. Princeton University Press.

10 W. Davies (2015). *The Happiness Industry: How the Government and Big Business Sold Us WellBeing*. London: Verso.

11 C. Taylor (1989). *Sources of the Self: The Making of the Modern Identity*. Cambridge University Press.

12 D. Anyfantakis et al. (2015). Effect of religiosity/spirituality and sense of coherence on depression within a rural population in Greece. *BMC Psychiatry* 15, p. 173.

13 T. B. Smith et al. (2003). Religiousness and depression: evidence for a main effect and the moderating influence of stressful life events. *Psychological Bulletin* 129, pp. 614–36.

14 Y. Chida et al. (2009). Religiosity/spirituality and mortality: a systematic quantitative review. *Psychotherapy and Psychosomatics* 78, pp. 81–90.

15 D. Myers (2008). Religion and human flourishing. In M. Eid and R. J. Larsen (eds.), *The Science of Subjective Well-Being*. New York: Guilford Press.

16 J. Son and J. Wilson (2011). Religiosity, psychological resources, and physical health. *Journal for the Scientific Study of Religion* 50, pp. 588–603.

17 C. J. Bennett and C. J. Einolf (2017). Religion, altruism, and helping strangers: a multilevel analysis of 126 countries. *Journal for the Scientific Study of Religion* 56, pp. 323–41.

18 A man of the cloth whom I know told me, quite rightly, that we should not believe in order to be happy but to become blissful – and that bliss is hardly an experience in line with happiness.

May

1   B. Bryson (2003). *A Brief History of Nearly Everything.* New York: Doubleday.
2   N. D. Tyson (2017). *Astrophysics for People in a Hurry.* New York: W.W. Norton, p. 18.
3   Otto's famous 1917 text about the holy is available at: https://archive.org/details/in.ernet.dli.2015.262513.
4   Neil deGrasse Tyson (2007). The cosmic perspective. *Natural History Magazine* April, pp. 193–4.
5   H. B. Nielsen and J. K. Rathje (2019). *Teorien om alt.* Copenhagen: Gyldendal.
6   Nielsen and Rathje, *Teorien om alt*, p. 206.
7   N. H. Gregersen (1997). Skabelsestro og evolutionsteori. In N. H. Gregersen (ed.), *Naturvidenskab og livssyn.* Copenhagen: Munksgaard, p. 264.
8   Gregersen, Skabelsestro og evolutionsteori, p. 267.
9   Gregersen, Skabelsestro og evolutionsteori, p. 295.

June

1   L. Wittgenstein (2009). *Philosophical Investigations* [1953] (bilingual edn). Chichester: Wiley-Blackwell, p. 179.
2   This distinction between 'participant' and 'spectator' is explained in Hans Skjervheim (1957). *Deltakar og tilskodar.* Oslo University Press.
3   S. Brinkmann (2014). Sjælen. In H.-J. Schanz (ed.), *50 ideer der ændrede verden.* Aarhus Universitetsforlag.
4   M. Hägglund (2019). *This Life: Secular Faith and Spiritual Freedom.* New York: Anchor Books.
5   The example is from C. Taylor (2002). *Varieties of Religion Today.* Cambridge, MA: Harvard University Press.

July

1   S. A. Kierkegaard (2008). *The Sickness unto Death* [1849]. Harmondsworth: Penguin. www.religion-online.org/book/the-sickness-unto-death.

2   I extrapolate on this in S. Brinkmann, *Standpoints: 10 Old Ideas in a New World* [originally in Danish, 2016]. Cambridge: Polity, 2018.

3   Also covered in Brinkmann, *Standpoints*.

4   K. Keefer (2008). *The New Testament as Literature*. Oxford University Press.

5   I. Ulbæk (2017). *Tro og tvivl: Selv ateister kan trænge til lidt gud*. Copenhagen: Akademisk Forlag, p. 272.

6   Keefer, *The New Testament as Literature*, p. 20.

7   S. A. Kierkegaard (1995). *The Concept of Anxiety* [1844]. Princeton University Press.

8   J. Katz (1996). The social psychology of Adam and Eve. *Theory & Society* 25, pp. 545–82, 557.

9   Katz, The social psychology of Adam and Eve, pp. 559–60.

10 Katz, The social psychology of Adam and Eve, p. 549.

11 Luke 10.37.

12 Luke 10.29.

13 This reading comes from Keefer, *The New Testament as Literature*.

14 Matthew 5.44–8.

15 J. Derrida (2001). *On Cosmopolitanism and Forgiveness*. London: Routledge, p. 32.

16 For more on this, see the analysis in Brinkmann, *Standpoints*, from which I have recycled some of the passages here.

17 Matthew 5.44.

18 S. Brinkmann (2021). *Vi er det liv, vi lever*. Copenhagen: Politikens Forlag.

19 H. Arendt (1977). *The Life of the Mind*. San Diego: Harcourt, p. 66.

20 Genesis 22.7–8.

21 Genesis 22:15–17.
22 The wording is from S. Critchley (2012). *The Faith of the Faithless*. London: Verso.
23 Keefer asks this question in his book on the New Testament as literature.

August

1 H. C. Peoples, P. Duda and F. W. Marlowe (2016). Hunter-gatherers and the origins of religion. *Human Nature* 27, pp. 261–82.
2 H. Dreyfus and S. D. Kelly (2011). *All Things Shining: Reading the Western Classics to Find Meaning in a Secular Age*. New York: The Free Press.
3 Dreyfus and Kelly, *All Things Shining*, p. 62
4 Dreyfus and Kelly, *All Things Shining*, p. 84.
5 Dreyfus and Kelly, *All Things Shining*, p. 194.

September

1 C. Seale (1998). *Constructing Death: The Sociology of Dying and Bereavement*. Cambridge University Press, p. 8.
2 E. Becker (2011). *The Denial of Death* [1973]. London: Souvenir Press.
3 For example, in the 2020 book *Grief: The Price of Love*. Cambridge: Polity.
4 I also quoted this fine poem in S. Brinkmann (2018), *Standpoints: 10 Old Ideas in a New World* [originally in Danish, 2016]. Cambridge: Polity.
5 See A. Sköld (2020). Being-towards-grief: rethinking death awareness. *Mortality* 26, pp. 284–98.
6 The points made below are from my chapter 'Sorg: Det umuliges kunst' (Sorrow: The Art of the Impossible), published in the 2021 anthology *Menneskets sorg* (Human Sorrow), ed. S. Brinkmann and A. Petersen. Aarhus: Klim.

7 H. Ruin (2018). *Being with the Dead: Burial, Ancestral Politics, and the Roots of Historical Consciousness.* Stanford University Press, p. 118.
8 This poem was translated into English by Susanna Nied and is available at: www.soerenulrikthomsen.dk/sut/trans lations/english/ShakenMirror.pdf.
9 N. M. Aidt (2017). Har døden taget noget fra dig så giv det til bage – Carls bog. Copenhagen: Gyldendal.
10 J. Didion (2005). *A Year of Magical Thinking.* London: Fourth Estate.
11 L. Ullmann (2015). *De urolige.* Copenhagen: Gyldendal.
12 C. Rørth (2019). *Hvad døden har lært mig om livet: 21 personlige fortæl linger.* Copenhagen: Kristeligt Dagblads Forlag.
13 J. Derrida (2001). *The Work of Mourning.* University of Chicago Press.
14 E. Levinas (1969). *Totality and Infinity: An Essay on Exteriority.* Pittsburgh: Duquesne University Press.
15 K. M. Guldager (2018). *Bjørnen.* Copenhagen: Gyldendal, p. 79.
16 Ruin, *Being with the Dead*, p. 201.
17 S. Critchley (2010). *How to Stop Living and Start Worrying: Conversations with Carl Cederström.* Cambridge: Polity, p. 40.
18 S. Critchley (2019). *Tragedy, the Greeks and Us.* London: Profile Books.
19 Critchley, *Tragedy*, p. 34.
20 Naja Marie Aidt's (2019) *When Death Takes Something from You Give It Back*, trans. Denise Newman.
21 Clifford Geertz (1966). *Religion as a Cultural System.* London: Tavistock, p. 4.
22 Aidt, *When Death Takes Something from You*, pp. 143–4.
23 G. Becker et al. (2007). Do religious or spiritual beliefs influence bereavement? A systematic review. *Palliative Medicine* 21, pp. 207–17.
24 J. H. Wortmann and C. L. Park (2008). Religion and

spirituality in adjustment following bereavement: an integrative review. *Death Studies* 32, pp. 703–36.
25 D. B. Feldman, I. C. Fischer and R. A. Gressis (2016). Does religious belief matter for grief and death anxiety? Experimental philosophy meets psychology of religion. *Journal of the Scientific Study of Religion* 55, pp. 531–9.
26 S. A. Lee, L. B. Roberts and J. A. Gibbons (2013). When religion makes grief worse: negative religious coping as associated with maladaptive emotional response patterns. *Health, Religion & Culture* 16, pp. 291–305.
27 *Berlingske Tidende*, 28 January 2020.

October

1 I. Ulbæk (2017). *Tro og tvivl: Selv ateister kan trænge til lidt gud.* Copenhagen: Akademisk Forlag, p. 228.
2 J. Sløk (1986). *Me and Godot: Memories.* Copenhagen: Downtown, p. 11.
3 Y. H. Harari (2017). *Homo Deus: A Brief History of Tomorrow.* London: Vintage.
4 See, for example, David Budtz Pedersen's analysis in (2019) 'Homo deus'. In F. Collin, D. B. Pedersen and F. Stjernfelt (eds.), *Menneskebilleder: Et analyseredskab.* Copenhagen: Hans Reitzels Forlag.
5 https://hpluspedia.org/wiki/Transhumanist_Declaration #March_1998_version_.282.1.29.
6 In his 1974 book *Anarchy, State and Utopia* (New York: Basic Books), the philosopher Robert Nozick discussed this as an 'experience machine', although he rejected the idea that people would be tempted by such a prospect.
7 https://singularityhub.com/2009/04/29/transcendent-man wows-at-tribeca-film-festival-premier.
8 The analysis of *Westworld* builds on a piece I wrote for *Politiken* on 17 December 2016.

November

1 S. Harris (2006). *Letter to a Christian Nation*. New York: Vintage Books.
2 However, this need not be the case. For example, Ib Ulbæk has written quite insightfully about God from an atheistic perspective. See I. Ulbæk (2017). *Tro og tvivl: Selv ateister kan trænge til lidt gud*. Copenhagen: Akademisk Forlag.
3 J. Hoffmeyer (2017). *7 ting vi plejer at tro på*. Copenhagen: Tiderne Skifter.
4 H. Arendt (1998). *The Human Condition* [1958]. University of Chicago Press, p. 279.
5 S. A. Kierkegaard (2008). *The Sickness unto Death* [1849]. Harmondsworth: Penguin.

December

1 H. J. Schanz (2017). *Ånd*. Aarhus: Klim.
2 S. U. Thomsen (2016). En hårnål klemt inde bag panelet: No ter fra eftertiden. Copenhagen: Gyldendal, p. 30.
3 H. Arendt (1977). *The Life of the Mind*. San Diego: Harcourt, p. 145.